"Yesterday I was clever, so I wanted to change the world.
Today I am wise, so I am changing myself."

- Rumi

STANDING CYCLIST

Flirting with Wisdom, One Breath,
One Mile at a Time

Frank Angelo Cavaluzzi

thirtythree45
MEDIA GROUP

Published by ThirtyThree45 Media Group. New York. First Edition.

ISBN-10: 0-692-83557-1
ISBN-13: 978-0-692-83557-9

Cover photo by Laura Wanderling. Montana photos by Kathy Henry. Mesothelioma Challenge photos by Courtney Davis and Danelle Mangone.

Several names have been changed to protect the privacy of those individuals and their families.

All of the authors and non-profit organizations mentioned herein own and maintain their own trademarks and copyrights, respectively, all of which should be noted and honored when reading this book. This includes, but is not limited to, the Mesothelioma Applied Research Foundation, Feeding America, and Stand Up To Cancer. LIVESTRONG is a registered trademark of The LIVESTRONG Foundation. Stand Up To Cancer and Stand Up To Cancer Brand Marks are registered trademarks of the Entertainment Industry Foundation (EIF). The author claims no employment, mutual representation or commercial allegiance with regards to the aforementioned organizations.

The author in no way encourages the modification of stock bicycles or the riding of bicycles standing up without a seat, on or off road. Regarding the treatment of Asthma and management of Asthma symptoms, this book recognizes the importance of medication in many cases and simply provides various methods and lifestyle modifications the author has personally found to be beneficial. Many of the activities depicted in this book can be considered dangerous and should not be attempted by children and untrained individuals.

Please always ride mindfully. Roll with great respect for our natural world. Be courteous to those around you, whether they be on wheels, on foot or on horseback. Lastly, please always ride with a helmet. Your comfort (or vanity) is simply not worth the risk of a brain injury.

To my dear parents, Frank and Marie Cavaluzzi, and everyone else in the world who live from a place of unconditional love, service and sacrifice. True altruism in action. I remain a humble student of your natural wisdom and aspire to live my own life in alignment with your values and virtues. Boundless peace and love to you all.

WORDS OF GRATITUDE

Many thanks to all of the hundreds of people I have met along every journey mentioned in this book, many of whom struggle with horrendous physical and emotional challenges. Your positive recognition of my own relatively minor accomplishments and seemingly endless encouragement has helped me heal and roll on, mile after mile. You are my heroes.

Thank you to all of those outstanding charitable organizations I have come to discover as a Standing Cyclist. Thanks for your remarkable, often underestimated, work that you do each year for millions of suffering people around the world. You are my champions.

Thank you to my sponsors and partners whose support and understanding make it possible for me to do what I do. You are my invaluable benefactors.

Thank you to all those special friends and literary collaborators who helped review and edit my early manuscript. You helped bring this book to life. You are my creative conscience.

Lastly, many thanks to all my dear family members and friends who have stood by me patiently with great love, year after year, through many ups and downs. Without you, I wouldn't be standing here today. You are my strength.

"Hey, stand-up guy! Go, go, go! You can do it!" I turned my head awkwardly toward the source of the hubbub, while carefully trying to maintain my pace. It was coming from a mammoth SUV filled with a pack of excited children in the back and two equally stoked adults at the helm. Collectively, in my mind, they represented family, friends, supporters, survivors and others that didn't make it through. I'm there with them, for them and because of them, I thought. I tried to see their faces, really see them, but the salty sweat puddling in my eyes burned away the shifting images. They yelled out questions but I couldn't hear very well over the roar of road traffic and the rapid pounding of my beating heart inside my ears. I wanted to cross the road, take a break, and say hello. I wanted to thank them for their support but I knew if I had stopped moving, that my weary legs and arms would likely seize up and I might not be able to continue on. I was only halfway through my day with another 20 miles to go. Any further delay and I would arrive at my overnight destination well after dark. If I pushed too hard to make up lost time, I might run out of energy, just short of my daily goal. I wanted to at least wave but it's risky riding my loaded touring bicycle with one hand while standing up, even for a moment. Of course, I have no seat to fall back on. When I release one hand from my handlebar, only one hand and two feet remain connected to maintain control over my sometimes uncooperative rig. I risk falling into traffic, injury or worse. There was no room for complications. I had to finish my 400-mile tour around Lake

Champlain, and I had to finish the way I began - riding the entire route standing up, without the ability to sit, to help bring attention to Stand Up To Cancer. They weren't the first posse of "fans" to find me that day. Apparently, more had seen the television coverage of my journey which aired the night before. It had brought out many special people with beautiful stories and kind words to share. They were pushing me forward past the fear, self-doubt and physical pain that surrounded my unusual endeavor. I stopped for some but could not for all. I had to be mindful of my pace and heart rate to help keep my Allergic Asthma in check. I couldn't risk an incident under those circumstances. I had to remain balanced, focused and roll on. Mile after mile, I repeated silently to myself, over and over, "There's still much to do. There's still much to do."

Based upon a journal entry by Frank A. Cavaluzzi
Near Plattsburgh, New York
September 18, 2009

CONTENTS

PREFACE

In cycling, a Century ride is a 100-mile (or more) single riding session, sometimes supported by helpful volunteers providing water, food and spare parts along the way. Other times, not so much, and you find yourself way out there on your own. A Century spans numerous regions and takes many hours to complete. Some hardcore endurance athletes may even attempt a double Century. The inevitable uphill grinds can be exhausting and even painful. Then there are the rolling hills and descents where we glide through the cool air, appreciate passing scenery, and enjoy the camaraderie of the group.

Much like life itself, a Century is a wild ride. Ups, downs, curves, close calls, breakdowns and repairs. It's full of anxiety, equanimity, resolve and fulfillment. This book is filled with much of the same. It is a glimpse of the challenges and triumphs of one simple soul. My own journey from confused racer, to disabled Asthma patient, to Standing Cyclist. From a dead end, self-oriented mindset to an ever-evolving heart space of compassion and service. Part memoir, part adventure cycling travelogue, prepared and presented like a multicourse meal of external exploration and self-inquiry. A tasty mix, I trust, with a little indigestion along the way. Crafted mindfully, with love, for athletes and entry level seekers and students as a stepping stone toward a greater understanding of who we truly are and why we do what we do.

INTRODUCTION

Some of us who refer to ourselves as cyclists rise early to train before sunrise, weigh our food and bicycle components, and worship racing. We must compete to feel whole and win to be happy. We must find ourselves leading the breakaway, or worst case drafting close behind. That was me, as a young man. At least that's who I thought I was. Soon it was clear that in the role of competitor, put plainly...I sucked. Eventually, I became that guy who would spend late nights with good friends then skip out on my high intensity AM training sessions. Not due to a lack of discipline, I can assure you. It was something far more fundamental than that.

I began to recognize that I had a deep aversion to any sort of serious competition. I was a poor performer, as a teen athlete, because deep down inside I lacked the drive to measure myself using others as my reference point. The concept of feeling good by beating someone else who themselves desperately wanted and needed to be first, turned me off, even though the societal framework surrounding me dictated otherwise. Gradually, I shifted away from the idea of racing.

My true passion was the drifting and discovery that came along with just simply riding a bike. Any kind of bike, anywhere. Short rides, long rides. With friends, strangers or solo. On-road, off-road. Camping out under the stars or crashing at cozy Bed & Breakfasts. The details didn't matter much. For me, it came down to freedom, forward motion and direct experience. The ability to wander and learn about life, and others, on my own terms. Yet at times to my detriment, I was far too restless yearning for all I was still missing, but always moving along with good intentions.

This simple wanderlust lifestyle soon advanced to include extreme ambition, egocentric indulgences and generally bad behavior. I was developing an image that others around me could identify with and reinforce, whether they realized it or not. Living this new supercharged life was touching me at my core, defining me as a person and all was well. Or so I thought, at the time, when I stopped long enough to think at all. Looking back, I was clearly preoccupied and self-centered. I can see now that my own self-crafted storyline, both consciously and unconsciously, impacted my energy and influenced my decisions at work and in my personal world to a significant degree.

It's difficult to enjoy a broader, objective view of all things when focused only on your own fun machine. Not a bad approach to life, for a while to some extent I suppose, but nothing so one dimensional can last forever. Eventually, our external reality catches up with our inner story, in one way or another. It could be the burst of responsibility accompanying the birth of a child or perhaps a shocking layoff from a job well worked for decades. For me, among other things, it was the grueling loss of loved ones and my own disabling loss of breath. It all screamed, "Pay attention. Wake up. There's more going on here. Let's get started." It forced a course correction, recharge and a new focus on a wider more balanced view of everything. A bigger, universal scene that didn't necessarily have me sitting at the center-point. Suddenly, for the first time, I felt small, vulnerable and directionless but incredibly clear and boundless as well. I was experiencing a vast openness to whatever insight and transformation lay ahead.

Some say our lives are journeys consisting of two different stages with varying points of overlap and inescapable setbacks. Earlier in life, we tend to be all-about-us. Somewhat melodramatic and self-absorbed. Immersed in our own triumphs and suffering. Our energy leans toward surviving, striving, building, craving, collecting, comparing and fluffing our feathers. At some point, we may begin to identify with what lies beyond who we think we are. We begin to see past the ego, or our own personal sense of self, into the connectedness and oneness of all things. A potentially blissful yet often painful transcendence.

What if there was an ethereal switch we could flip to help us wake up permanently from our own story without doing all the required work along the way? If there was such a switch, would we know to flip it? Would we actually choose to flip it? Should we choose to flip it? Must we first spin and fall on our own, again and again, before rising to new levels? Do we have to experience the truths in life, firsthand, before we're capable of big picture living? Through direct experience, not only by reading books and scriptures or listening to lectures and sermons, but by actually navigating the intricacies of daily existence with full attention. Sitting with and moving through the many perceived ups and downs, with great mindfulness. I don't mean to get ahead of myself. Please keep these questions and notions in mind as you move through this chronicle of adventures and reflections, and decide for yourself.

PART ONE

Chapter 1 - THE STARTING LINE

We all have an earliest memory from our childhood. My earliest was being placed inside my cousin Vilma's purse. I vaguely remember looking up from the bottom surface of her seemingly giant handbag. I could see a bright white light and Vilma's smiling face way up above at the opening. I could feel the sensation of movement as she walked around the room, her purse bouncing along on her shoulder. I found out, when I was much older, that Vilma had been joking about taking me home with her and that I was giggling and shaking with joy at the idea.

Even at a young age, I was always wanting to move. I wasn't happy unless I was traveling from one place to another. I always felt most at home when away from home. I couldn't wait to take trips with my father in his pristine vintage 1967 Ford Galaxie 500. It was a fairly rare, huge, black sedan with tall rounded fenders, classic chrome accents and deep cushioned seats. I took my traditional place in the front passenger seat, while my mother sat in the back. It became a family joke. Something about my mom getting chauffeured around. I didn't care where I sat, as long as I remained in motion. I remember seeing an old Super 8 home movie of my father holding me high in the air while I swirled my legs violently for long periods of time, like a spinning motor, or as if I was peddling with a purpose. Much like other kids, I was always riding Big Wheels, tricycles and anything else I could self-propel, often right into the perfect plastic covered Italian provincial furniture inside my parents' Bronx, New York apartment, where I was raised for the first nine years of my life.

My grandparents owned a modest cottage in the Catskills. It sat in a tidy upstate New York mountain community called Wurtsboro Hills. We had spent many memorable weekends and summers up there. My Grandma Stella had been sick for years and now I was watching my Grandpa Angelo go in and out of the hospital far too often for my young heart to bear. I was six when he died. Months later, my mother's family graciously offered to turn over my grandparents' bungalow to my parents so we could leave the city and they could raise me in the country environment I had grown to love so much. In the Bronx, we lived across the street from a rowdy pub and upstairs from a classic NYC pizza joint. Frequent bar fights and local break-ins sealed the deal for our move.

One summer, not long before we lost Angelo, he had given my parents the money to buy me my first bicycle. I was anxious to try my luck and test my skills on two wheels. I soon learned how to ride my grandpa's gift across the thick grass of our front lawn, minus the training wheels. My mom ran alongside me, back and forth, hour after hour, until I could maintain my balance on my own, without face planting in the grass. Something very special happened to me in that moment, when she first let go and I rolled off on my own. A seed had been planted. A seed that would be watered daily, in the years to come.

Our rural upstate community was laced with dirt roads, dense woods, and filled mostly with small cottages sporting homegrown, handyman additions. The kids in the neighborhood were a healthy mix of tough Brooklyn, Queens, and Bronx transplants, and country born and raised roughnecks. Hanging out aimlessly, day and night, became our favorite pastime. We'd wander our narrow roads, we called trails, with our bicycles, sharing city stories, daydreaming and cooking up trouble. There were only a few street lights on the entire mountain, so when the sun set, we learned to navigate the trails intuitively. No one had any money for flashlights. Besides, that would have taken the fun out of it. This sixth-sense GPS would prove useful later in life, when my itchy feet would lead me well beyond the Catskills into the Rockies, Utah's Canyonlands, to Iceland and other remote locations. When we'd get bored of walking and riding, we'd sit right in the middle of whatever road we happened to be on at the time and we wouldn't move. Passing cars were forced to weave around us often brushing past sharp branches and deep drainage ditches in the process. A bold, mindless move, but hey, we owned those roads. It was our mountain. We were THE center of the universe and considered ourselves bulletproof in every sense of the word.

Back in the late 1970's, my close friends and I would take our department store bikes out into the woods, as I'm sure many kids had, well before mountain biking was an official sport. Flying through tight, homemade single-track strands behind our friend Bryan Stanton's house, we discovered an intense rush and a new purpose. We began spending our days and nights grooming trails, building jumps, and practicing stunts. This is back when BMX racing was taking off and in that arena Bryan was the best around. He was fearless, skillful, and as tough as nails. He was my earliest inspiration to push myself beyond who I thought I was, on and off two wheels. In gym class, Bryan always ran laps, way out in front, seemingly with great ease. My flat feet, weak ankles and growing belly were usually flapping along at the back. He always had the girls chasing him and the guys envying him. But Bryan never made me or anyone else feel inadequate. He never saw himself as better or cooler. He was just another one of our pack, passing time and having fun. We always saw Bryan as thriving but in reality, beyond the scenes, he was struggling to survive. Bryan had been ill with severe Kidney Disease beginning back when he was a young boy. It never held him back until around puberty. If it had, we couldn't tell. After that, his health problems took their toll, eventually ending his life far too early. Over the years, he and I had lost touch. That was more my doing than his. Throughout my twenties, my work, adventures, relationships and rewards took center stage. I couldn't fathom what he was going through, so I suppose I pushed it out of my life entirely. Perhaps it was easier to move on than dig in deep and upset my own flow. I grew to deeply regret this and continue to reflect upon it, to this day.

When I was about thirteen, my good friend Joe Russo and I set off on our first significant long distance ride, with our heavy steel "high-end" road bikes. Our route ran along a rural yet busy interstate highway which ran from the village of Wurtsboro to the little Ulster County village of Ellenville, just south of Minnewaska State Park and the well-known Mohonk Mountain House resort near New Paltz, NY. Some say those long, dark historic hotel hallways laced with old portraits of famous guests dating back to the early 1900's, was Stephen King's inspiration when envisioning the fictitious Overlook Hotel from the best-selling novel, *The Shining.*

This was a milestone journey for us. It was only about 26 miles round trip, but for us at the time, it may as well have been a Century ride. Breathing in the newfound freedom that comes along with any distance ride, we felt like a million bucks. Well, that is, until I made my mark...on the pavement. A big bloody mark. We had just rolled into Ellenville and were transitioning from relatively wide, flat shoulders to busy, narrow streets with hefty curbs. I had been riding a few minutes ahead of Joe, who was just out of sight behind me. I hadn't the confidence to brave the busy streets so I decided to hop the curb and illegally ride the sidewalk to avoid the next several nasty blocks of traffic. The problem was, I never hopped. No hop, no slowdown, just a full speed sideswipe. Needless to say, it didn't end well. I found myself face up, covered in pebbles and blood. Human sandpaper. My eyeglasses and one shoe were missing. After my head stopped spinning, I realized the missing shoe was still strapped into one of my old fashioned toe clip pedals on my twisted machine, which landed about 15 feet away from my launch. A gang of nearby teenagers, just hanging around town, ran over to check out the scene. A tough looking bunch but they meant well. They stood supportively around me, searched for my missing eyeglasses, and tried helping me up. Just then, Joe rounded the corner and spotted the bloody mess and mangled metal. He immediately jumped to conclusions and figured that my new friends had decked me and were stealing my bike, cash and whatever else. He jumped off his bike and immediately went into attack mode. Joe went full tilt Brooklyn on those Good Samaritans disguised as country punks. I was trying to explain what had happened but nothing was going to stop him. He chased them down the street, screaming and swearing. Quite funny actually. Joe was always saving me, even into adulthood. I would mindlessly start trouble, and he would find himself on the receiving end of the fallout.

The ride home was filled with Band-Aids and big laughs about our first tale as true cyclists. We were now officially roadies. We couldn't wait to get home to share our accomplishment, and the drama, with our friends. Our parents, well that's a different story entirely. Needless to say, our interstate highway antics did not go over well. We could hear Joe's dad yelling all the way from our house, which sat 2 blocks away from his. A roar which almost always instantly earned me a grounding from my own dad simply by association, if for no other more substantial reason.

Over the next year, I spent many days and some nights logging many miles, alone. Most of my friends were shifting their focus to dirt bikes, quads and other motorized toys. I knocked off day rides through my beautiful Catskill foothills, in between shifts at the local grocery store and evening dishwasher duties at the secluded restaurant which sat at the top of the mountain near my home in Wurtsboro Hills. A fancy gourmet hideaway frequented by the Rat Pack, and their glamorous ladies, way back in the early Catskill heydays.

I was spending most of my time daydreaming about high school girls I would never date, my first car (which I was still saving up for), and of course my dream bike. I had built and rebuilt that bike in my mind, many times over. I would ride around with an old Palo Alto Bicycle mail order catalog in the back pocket of my jersey and when I'd stop to rest or have lunch, I'd pull it out for inspiration. I would visualize all of the ultralight components and clever bike tools I would order. I learned how to build and fix bicycles from reading that catalog, long before ever touching a spanner or Allen wrench. I would drool over pictures of perfectly staged, masterfully crafted Campagnolo cranksets and vintage Brooks hard leather saddles. I'd get butterflies in my stomach whenever a new edition arrived in my mailbox. Then, disaster struck. The plug was pulled. I hadn't bought anything since I started receiving these catalogs so the company stopped mailing them to me, rightfully, to save money no doubt. I used my extra time to do more riding and less dreaming.

My fifteenth year was full of friends, seemingly endless fun and many near misses. My most memorable involved a huge bull on a winding backcountry streetcar route called Glen Wild Road near Rock Hill, NY. I had come up behind a long line of cars that appeared to be waiting for something. I anxiously rode up around the cars to find traffic backed up in both directions, held in limbo by several cows and two tremendous bulls standing in the middle of the road. Now for me this was something special. I was still fairly new to upstate living and, needless to say, there was no livestock down in my old Bronx neighborhood. On the bike, I was Superman, so fear had not entered into the equation. I stood right up next to the lead cars and boldly taunted the frisky animals. Just then, I heard the voice of an angel. Actually, it was a busty blond I referred to as Angel. She was stretched out in her shiny 280Z coupe at the head of the pack of gridlocked vehicles. We got to chatting and me being 15, teeming with testosterone, I hung on every word. She crafted a plan that would move us both past the danger zone. Angel would drive forward slowly with me riding along the right side of her sharp little red sports car. We'd pass the cows and grouchy bulls safely, she'd think I was the shit, and I'd have another great story to come home with. My growing, high octane ego was loving the idea. Bad plan. Soon after she got moving, one of the bulls turned and looked her square in the eyes. Her car sat lower than his head, which added to this already intimidating scenario. Next thing I knew, she had nailed the gas, screeched off ahead, and I was left coasting alongside this now highly irritated brute. I had been chased by dogs before but this was entirely different. I started sprinting, upshifting rapidly every few seconds, looking back along the way to find my new friend breathing heavy, busting forward, right behind me. Now at times like this, you would think your life would pass before your eyes. You would be overcome with terror. You'd imagine crashing and being stomped to death by this cow chasing King Kong. Not me. All I could ponder was Angel and her big blond 80's hair, pink tank top and compelling perfume disappearing up over the hill ahead. Maybe I could still catch her, I thought.

As my youthful overconfidence, often arrogance, grew so did my collection of stories and lessons. On one training day in particular, a day at times I would prefer to forget, I was soaring down Wild Turnpike Road near Wanaksink Lake, NY on my road bike, about 5 miles away from my house, passing the many construction signs placed along the roadway. I ignored the warnings and proceeded with even greater gusto. There were now flaggers and construction workers visible and instead of politely slowing down out of respect and to avoid striking them, I dodged them (barely) like lifeless obstacle course cones, blowing off their warnings and returning their obscenities. Then, Karmic cause-and-effect reared its head. I came around a blind corner where more workers were patching long sections of the road with hot tar. I was riding way too fast to stop suddenly. I went into autopilot mode, maintained pace, and motored through it. I could tell from their faces and middle fingers they were both worried and angry (mostly angry), as the tar flew up from the road surface, striking them, coating my face, bare legs, fancy yellow cycling jersey, and my bright white bicycle frame. It was only hot for a moment but I knew the real problem would be the tar getting inside my moving bicycle parts. By the time I made it home to my parents' house, I could barely shift or brake. I knocked on the door and my little white haired Italian mother Marie answered. Ree was used to me getting myself into unusual messes, on and off the bike, so she wasn't terribly surprised or worried but she certainly had no intention of letting me in "her kitchen" like that. Only then did I realize just how bad it was. I was covered from head to toe with tar. I had to strip down in the yard and scrub my body with kerosene and a heavy duty bristle brush. It was all fun and games up until that moment. The burning sores, aching bruises and ripping scabs would later remind me just how painful being a butthead could be.

That autumn brought another dangerous adventure into my life. My first official girlfriend. She lived 15 miles away, over a mountain, just past my High School in Monticello, NY. Monticello sat in the heart of Sullivan County, a Catskill region known for legendary resort hotels such as The Concord, Grossinger's and of course the famous 60's Woodstock music festival in Bethel, not far from my girlfriend's home. I didn't have a license or car yet so driving to see her wasn't an option. Cycling would become my savior. I would rise early, around 4am, gear up and head out on my bike before most people in my neighborhood even opened their eyes. That doesn't sound so unusual today but back in the 80's, it was much less common, at least in that region. I was certainly considered an oddball. The ride to school kicked off with an isolated wooded 6-mile road ascent, some flats, and then steep rolling hills up and over a local ski area. It would take me about 1 ½ hours to get there, riding up out of the saddle most of the time. I always enjoyed standing on hills. I couldn't get enough of it.

After rolling into school, I'd shower quickly in the gym locker-room, then slide into homeroom just in time to start the day. After school I'd ride the extra 3 miles from school to my girlfriend's house, spend some quality time together, then ride back home over the mountain usually before nightfall. But not always, sometimes relying on a tiny Radio Shack flashlight taped to my handlebar or helmet, and the misty glow of the moon to find my way. This routine built muscle, burned off traditional baked ziti Sunday dinners, and increased my endurance. I was crafting a strong foundation, but didn't see it that way at the time. I was in it for the open road and teen love.

I was never really a team sport kind of guy. I tried but could never really make it work. At one point in High School, I joined the wrestling team. That didn't last. Practice was too rigid for my tastes and matches were unnerving. I couldn't find the fun in organized, team sports. I just wanted to ride. I wanted to roll with good friends, but more often than not, still found myself rolling alone. When I had the time to go out exploring, they didn't. Also, by then, most had traded in their two wheelers for four-wheel drive trucks and red convertibles. They could cover more miles, with beer, buddies and girlfriends in tow, without breaking a sweat. A motor did have its advantages but when my time came, I was more of a Ford Pinto kind of guy. Yes, I said Pinto. The revolutionary automobile known for blowing up when hit from behind. As long as I had a place to transport my bike and a few friends, I was good. It was around this time I caught the road racing bug. That bug sucked me in, chewed me up, and later spit me out in a big way.

Like many cyclists at the time, I was following Greg Lemond with a fervor comparable only to the cycling world's new millennium addiction to Lance and his cohorts. Heck, I thought I was Greg Lemond. I'd pretend to draft his contemporaries and at the very last moment, just before rounding the corner near my girlfriend's house, I would slingshot past them and nail the win by one droplet of sweat gliding down off the tip of my nose. I was amazing, I thought in my own mind. I needed to try my hand at the real thing.

I purchased a United States Cycling Federation (USCF) racing license, officially began my training, and searched out nearby sanctioned and unsanctioned races. I soon noticed that my age category was filled with younger riders who used all their spare time to train. They had no part-time jobs outside of school. I was working two, to support my bike, car and dating habits. These kids were all lean muscle and had the cardiovascular systems, and sheer will to win, of Olympic contenders. Me, not so much, which brings me to Team Frank.

Ultimately, I had discovered that a New York Empire State Games road race qualifier was being held about 1 hour away in Bear Mountain, NY. I registered to compete and lined up my buddy Brad for support. He would help organize my tools, food, spare parts and would drive my tan Pinto, our impressive official Team car, from the staging area to the finish line. I couldn't afford roof racks at the time so everything was haphazardly jammed through the back hatch, down across the folded rear seats.

It was my time to shine. I knew I was going to qualify. I was in. I had weighed my components and built up what I thought was a sleek racing machine. I had experience, I trained hard, I could talk the talk, and was sure I would ride the ride. At the starting line, some of us donned now ancient, soft leather strip helmets and positioned our feet for maximum launch. We rolled off in a dense pack but soon the pack broke into sections. There was the lead group, a middle group, a trailing pack and then there was me. Suddenly, I transformed from a world-class athlete, in my own imagination, to a slug struggling across a patio on a hot summer day, melting away one muscle contraction at a time. I could blame it on my choice of equipment, my few extra pounds, the humidity, or my elite competition but the bottom-line was, I didn't want it. Not like the other guys. Not even close. I was simply doing what I expected myself to do. I was fulfilling my own pack-minded expectations by joining a highly organized, group event that everyone else in the game thought was cool, so I would be cool. I was now an official competitor, on the record, like the rest, but felt more out of place than ever before.

All this rolled through my throbbing brain as I watched every last rider smoke me, then something clicked. I caught a tiny glimpse of who I really am. A peek at what sat just past the gobbledygook of my own storyline. This didn't last very long, but it did leave an enduring residue that would reanimate in later years. At that point, I thought seriously about quitting. I heard my parents' always supportive voices in my head say, "Hey, as long as you tried, that's all that matters." I knew I couldn't quit though. I needed to continue on, just to see if I could finish the race. I hunkered down, remembered my training, and readjusted my mindset. I was no longer out for that slot on the qualifying team. I began to enjoy the effort itself and all the glorious mountain scenery. One moment and one pedal stroke at a time. Fully present. I had suddenly and shockingly become a cycling purest. An enlightened roller or so it seemed.

I began to pick up speed and a huge rush came over me. Adrenaline soon displaced the calm mindful appreciation I had begun to adopt moments before and I got carried away carelessly into fantasies about my new improved headspace. I was no longer operating in the present moment, for 30 minutes or so I would guess. I was dreaming, lost in thoughts of future events and more meaningful accomplishments down the road, and brainlessly bombed the first sizeable downhill I had seen so far.

At first it was a mild descent but it soon steepened. I was approaching 45 MPH, heading into a tight corner, the first of two. I hit the first well. My line was good, pedal position safe, and body tucked down tight. Approaching the second, my eyes were watering as I swung my body and bike from the left to the right with confidence. Just then I could see the blur of a tree branch across the asphalt. I was moving too quickly and was leaning too hard for an evasive maneuver. It was instant. The hit, the slide, the burst of my skin along the roadway.

The whole event lasted seconds but felt like hours. I came to a stop in a heaping pile on the far side of the road, just off the shoulder. I had missed the guardrail by inches. As I sat up in a daze covered with blood, I considered what had just happened and took inventory as most seasoned cyclists do, post-crash. I hadn't broken any body parts although my pride, along with the skin on my forearms and knees, had been shaved a little thinner. I leaned over to untangle myself from my bike, which was still attached to my feet and soon realized that I hadn't hit a tree branch. I had spun out on a large Black Snake. It must have whipped up and tangled in my rear wheel as I crashed. All that remained of it was a severed head and some innards. My new olive green frame was coated in a combination of snake guts and my own blood. I remember thinking, in my stupor, that color combo looked kind of cool. Must have been the ding on the head. I then discovered my face and shoulder-length hair were also colored with reptile juice.

Just as I was freeing myself up and bending my wheel free from my frame's chainstays, a race vehicle came speeding up the road behind me. They barely slowed, yelled at me through the open window to get out of the way, and continued on. Yep, I so don't belong here, I thought. I finished picking snake parts and Frank parts from any important moving parts on the bike, then headed off to the finish line via a marked short-cut. My wheel was too badly bent to finish the race in any practical period of time. As I turned the final corner, limping along to the finish line, something happened that I would never experience again within this context. Crowds of people cheering, including my buddy Brad who was minding our Team Car, came running toward the finish line to greet me with candy and water in hand. I had won! Well, so they thought. I must admit, for a split second, the thought of throwing my arms up into the air crossed my mind. But of course I didn't. Would that have been worse than doping today? I wonder. In any case, I learned a lot that day. About myself up to that point, what's truly important, and about what really made me tick. Unfortunately, it was all soon forgotten. Most of it anyway, but life has a way of getting its point across, eventually, one way or another. If you don't learn the first time, or tenth time, guaranteed there will be an eleventh time coming your way. The universe is relentless. Thank God for that.

Of course I took my road bike to college with me. It was an inexpensive glossy red Italian import, at the time. I used to boast that even the air in the tires was Italian. I think I even used that as a pickup line once or twice. Yes, I had seen the classic 1979 cycling movie, *Breaking Away*, one too many times. Not much had changed since High School. I was still hooked on cycling, adventure, beer and girls. Sometimes I was fortunate enough to enjoy all four. Road trips were the best for this. Among other things, they helped to pacify my restless nature, at that time.

I'd go on college "daze" walkabouts or rideabouts with friends or alone, sometimes for days. Far too often, I'd even skip class to do it. I couldn't resist it. I was drawn to move and escape. On cold, quiet winter nights, a close friend and I would often drift for many miles along the dark roadside like hobos, stopping at 24 hour delis to order cold cut heros to soothe our cranky bellies. We'd walk through local used car lots to find any unlocked autos, hunker down inside, and would eat our overloaded submarine sandwiches well protected from the wind and snow. I would wander off alone with a small daypack, hiking along the Hudson River in upstate NY, near where I attended school. One evening at dusk, I bunked in the dirt at a construction site, nestled around a kerosene stove I found hidden under a tarp. I couldn't get enough of the solitude and the unknown.

I would intentionally register for a lot of evening classes and was becoming quite a night owl. I'd sleep part of the day away wherever I found myself, sometimes on the floor of dorm rooms, sometimes in my own apartment, then go to classes, do homework, work, and socialize through the night. Most people never saw me actually sleeping. I soon earned the nickname, The Bat. I'd cycle in between classes, parties and the two side jobs I worked to help pay my way through school.

One job was stocking shelves at a huge grocery store in Poughkeepsie, NY and the other was working for physically and medically challenged students at my college. The latter may well be the most important work I have ever done, to date. I didn't realize it at the time though. I attended classes with my clients, took notes for those who couldn't move, see or hear well, then helped tutor them after class. Among others, I worked for a quadriplegic band manager, a hearing impaired coed with a warped sense of humor (much like my own), a terminal AIDS patient and a legally blind boy with multiple personality disorders, each hell-bent on finishing school and earning their degree. I learned more from serving these persistent people than I did in all my own classes combined. But at the time, I was shallow, exhausted and confused. The deep value of that experience lingered in vague form. It would take me many years to fully recognize and truly connect with it on a heart level. I say confused because I was wedged in between these highly focused, persevering, inspired and inspiring individuals that I worked for, and my own classmate acquaintances some of whom didn't even want to be in school at all. Part of me was accepting of everyone's role and story but another part of me was angry. Why did some have it so hard and others take it all for granted. Also, I secretly resented having to work so hard to stay in school when many fellow students had it so easy. Some were there just to satisfy their parents and had no real interest in learning about anything in particular. Or maybe they were bored or restricted at home and this was their legitimate way out. One great friend of mine, truly built for fun, would have his parents send him book money and we'd spend much of it on booze. The deal was, if you needed $200 for books, you'd ask for $400. There was enough for both books and beverages, with some cash leftover for the occasional weekend getaway. Yes, I sometimes resented how hard I had it and how easy others appeared to have it, but envy, anger and confusion aside I had no problem spending their book money on road trips and small batch bourbon.

Chapter 2 - A GLIMPSE

After my time at school, I moved back to the Catskills to regroup and took a job with a high-tech startup company as a Field Engineer. I worked on equipment used in the manufacturing of computer chips at Texas Instruments, Intel and AMD. I lived on the road for almost 3 years, returning home only a couple of times every month or so, to party with my hometown buddies and to go out mountain biking. To stay in shape when out on the road, I would use hotel fitness centers whenever possible. However, after long days confined in environmentally controlled cleanroom labs, sealed up to my eyeballs in highly restrictive, bright white Tyvek jumpsuits, happy hours filled with cold beer and road friends would often win out. Instead of waking up sore from a great workout, I'd awake with a pounding hangover headache. I began to crave the outdoors more and more. I was drifting away from my core, and falling deeper into the mainstream, rat race. Yet another race I had no interest in winning. I was on my way to burning out. I knew it, but I was frozen in motion and couldn't do anything about it.

Eventually, I earned my way into an inside leadership position, got myself off the road and hit the woods, hard. I was mostly riding single-track and double-track mountain trails with local road riding falling in far behind. My stomping grounds became the cliffside trails at Minnewaska State Park and the secluded hardpack switchbacks at Mohonk, which sat adjacent. Both were part of the Shawangunk Mountain range. The Gunks were famous for rock climbing. Legends such as Lynn Hill put up classic routes and helped put The Gunks on the map as a world-class climbing destination. At one time, Chamonix in France, Yosemite and The Gunks were at the center of the climbing world.

On my now "too few" days off, I would disappear into those hills on my mountain bike, with my climbing shoes and chalk dust bag tied across my back. I would ride to isolated areas and test my skills at bouldering six to twelve feet overhangs. Climbing rock alone, unroped, and the meditative single point of focus required to do so successfully, was beginning to appeal to me almost as much as bombing through trees on two wheels. That climbing kind of motion and rhythm, like summertime ski resort downhill mountain biking, is an "all in" activity. A stray thought is not an option. You stray, and you're dead...or worse. Coma, a broken neck, etc. It's all more of a fully engaged series of movements than merely a recreational activity, when done correctly with the right intention. A meditation-in-motion, but back then it was still more about the rush than a glimpse of something bigger.

At one point, back around 1996, I realized two very important things about myself. I needed to exercise my creativity and I needed to spend more time in the natural world than inside artificially lit office cubes and HEPA filtered labs. I always had a sketch pad and calculator with me, even on long training rides and fly-away business trips. I found myself drafting everything from technical sportswear to bicycle components, and soon after, departed from my conventional role as a Project Leader and Operations Manager in a traditional company setting. Of all things, shoelaces turned out to be a noteworthy crossroads in both my career and outdoor lifestyle. One of my closest friends and business partner, Brian Salerno, and I had developed specialized bootlaces for Hiking, Trekking, Biking, Hockey and Snowboarding. They were a strategically designed weave of aramid fiber (the material used in bulletproof vests) and polyester, resulting in an easy to tie, well-knotted, super strong braid well matched to these aggressive outdoor activities. Our tagline was something like, "Designed to Outlast Your Boots" which proved to be quite true. Brian managed the operation while I mostly focused on product variations and field testing, along with Brian himself and several athletically inclined friends.

Looking back, it was a perfect life chapter. We were expressing ourselves creatively and I could spend the majority of my time traveling between trees. I would disappear for days, sometimes weeks, biking and hiking trails from West Virginia to Maine. Having little money at the time, bikepacking, backpacking and car camping became my nightly routine. Usually solo, I wandered through the mountains letting my mind run wild in whatever direction it needed to go. Brian and I would brainstorm new designs and applications, collaborate on paper and model our concepts. We would build wooden, fabric or scrap metal prototypes, utilizing whatever tools and resources we had at the time.

We sold small quantities of our laces to individuals and out-fitters throughout the United States and Canada, until we scored a big break with a top snowboard manufacturer. The big time or so we thought. The sample laces we had sent out tested very well in the industry and, within months, led to our first big private label sale. I can still remember that fat five figure check. We actually photocopied it before cashing it, as a souvenir I suppose. But that was the easy part. Now we needed to produce, wrap, package, stage (in customer supplied POP displays) and ship out thousands of pairs of laces.

It was time for me to come in off the trail to assist Brian with the real work. We got the job done with time to spare, thanks to helpful friends and family, my own girlfriend at the time, and a terrific production and assembly group we ended up partnering with. They were an NGO that employed a beautiful, local workforce of physically and mentally chal-lenged clients. Brian and I loved our check-in visits. We were always greeted with such warmth, kindness and excitement from both clients and staff. We were pleased to be growing our business and, at the same time, supporting highly fo-cused and passionate participants right in our own community.

We reinvested most of our laces profit into other designs and products which never really panned out. The sports in-dustry was changing its mode of operation. Most everything was now being sourced from China, except for Technical Project Management. We shifted our business over to a service-oriented model and used our skills and experience to lead development projects for client companies. A combination of low overhead and extreme flexibility made this the perfect configuration for both of us. I was able to head back into the mountains, but now I had the time and the money to do it well. I was no longer limited to East Coast exploration. I hungered for the thin air of the Rockies and great expanse of the high desert plains of Utah. Once I saw those high peaks in Summit County, Colorado just outside of Breckenridge and Vail, and felt the dirty grit in my teeth while cycling Moab's classic Porcupine Rim Trail, I knew I had found my new muse.

There's always been a part of me that considers the Colorado/Utah region my home. Maybe in a past life, maybe later in this life. Hard to say. It's been full of firsts for me. My first time above 14,000 feet (along with my first bout of altitude sickness). My first weeklong solo off-road bikepacking trip in the steaming hot desert single-track near Canyonlands National Park in Utah. I still have and use gear that is permanently stained with the red dirt of that region. Using it always brings great memories to mind. Memories like lying down, stargazing on a clear night. Sleeping out without a tent, 25 miles from the nearest living thing, not counting pointy cacti and the scorpions and snakes looking to snuggle inside my sleeping bag. I was fully invested in that lifestyle and loving it.

These trips back in the 90's gave me time to reflect. Sometimes, too much time. Not all the memories were good. Like when my mother, Ree, went through Cancer 10 years earlier. She survived but not due to any significant assistance from me. I was engrossed in my own world. I barely remember the details. My dad took great care of her and saw to her every need, while I hovered in my own immature bubble, focused mostly on my own relatively insignificant problems, goals, work and social life. I think many of those solo trips were forced reflections on this disconnect. A self-oriented existence that kept me from seeing and feeling what was really going on around me. It wasn't denial or delusion. It was disinterest. Disinterest in anything that did not directly involve me. I was sleepwalking (and sleep riding) through life. It would be years before I would even come close to waking up.

The days between January 2000 and December 2001 were blurry at best. My family and friends lost several good men, then, the Twin Towers tragedy on 9/11/01 which of course impacted the entire world. First, Don lost his battle with Cancer early in 2000. Don was an important cornerstone within our community of friends. He was a very special father and husband and his passing impacted all of us a great deal. Not long after, my mother and I lost my own father, suddenly, to a massive heart attack. We were blown apart. On top of that, only days before my father's death, my Godfather Jack, passed after a long and complicated illness. While still grieving our own personal losses, all so closely clustered together, we would soon face a gut wrenching terrorist attack that claimed the lives of many thousands in our tri-state area. A desperate and confusing act of violence that continues to traumatize every community affected to this very day, to some degree.

Those early days were certainly dark times and we all coped in our own way. For me, it was self-imposed isolation and wine. A bottle a night, at the very least. Good stuff, crap stuff, it didn't matter. I was shooting for numb and enough of most anything did the trick at that time. For the first 2 weeks after my father's passing, I didn't work at all. I stayed with my mom at her house. The house my dad had died in. The home I was raised in. Intentionally sleeping on the couch which sat four feet away from where my father had taken his last breath. During the day, I would manage the loss of our patriarch much like I would run a business. Make calls, sort through paperwork, and maintain the property. Each evening, my mom and I would sit together and reflect on what had happened, reliving each detail and every emotion.

I would listen carefully and try to view this loss through her eyes and heart, empathetically. Something I was not particularly skilled in, at that time. They were married 45 years when we lost my dad and they were as close to soul-mates as I believe any two people could be. I remember trying to absorb my mother's grief, to help ease her pain. When it worked, those were the hardest times for me. I'd like to think it helped, in some small way at least. In some subtle corner of myself, I didn't speak about, I myself knew the essence of my dad was intact and ok. I could feel it and this kept me going. However, this was far beyond my mom's current state of mind. She would begin to heal in time, but not today, I thought. Today, it's all on me and I would have to step up.

When she'd finally fall asleep, I would sit in the kitchen, just one small room away from my dad's last moments, and introduce myself to a tasty new bitter sweet bottle of red. My date for the evening. My friends, via telephone mostly, helped me through these dark days. A few very special friends in particular, I felt, actually kept me breathing when I was too drained and confused to bother. They are my family, I love them and I am forever in their debt.

During this time, I began to see life differently. It was more of a knowing I suppose. A glimpse past the rush and distraction of my own self-interest, into the bigger picture. Into the world around me. I was still spending time in the mountains, camping, bouldering, scrambling around with a pack or mountain biking, but now it was more contemplative. The adrenaline rush began to shift from dangling carrot to occasional side-effect. I would ride for 2 hours then sit on the edge of 100 foot cliffs, just breathing and staring off at the distant hills and valleys of the lower Catskills. Often, I would think about my dad, my Godfather Jack, my friend Don, the families of 9/11 victims and how all of our lives had changed so dramatically in such a relatively short period of time. I would look for logical connections and teachings buried within the cold, dark fog of loss and survivor's guilt. For hours, through wind, rain and snow, I would search but usually came up short. It wasn't a logical time for any of us. There were no straightforward answers for anyone to find. There was a lot of gray going around and acceptance seemed to be the only path to take, but it remained a challenging, technical path for everyone.

Thanks to my good friend George, and his lasting influence, I had learned to meditate years earlier but my practice was on-again, off-again up to this point. Now, I was returning to steady practice without even realizing it. My hours of reflecting while riding and sitting in the natural world was emptying me out until I just "was". I wasn't trying, it would just happen. I was still sleepwalking through my life but these little bits of awake time were slowly unfolding a new role for me. An authentic role that wasn't a role at all. I was seeing a small sliver of my natural state. Who I had been as a child, in my earliest recollections before life fully kicked in and influenced me in worldly ways. I began to recall afternoons in my preteen years, wandering off down nearby trails, where I would sit and stare at tree tops bending back and forth without breaking. Hypnotized by creeks trickling down the hillside, tickling my ears and sparking my imagination. For hours, I would flow like this until the gap between my fleeting thoughts would grow and feel like home. My true home. When I was a child, I thought this meant I was spacey and lazy. Now I think, to combat this belief, I had worked extra hard at my part-time jobs while growing up. Five hours turned into ten, then weekends and eventually long summer workdays monopolized my time and thoughts. I was a working man now, saving up money for a car so I could go out cruising. No time for mindless skygazing. I had entered the mainstream but hadn't really noticed. It's like the story about the frog and the boiling water. If you place a frog into a pot of boiling water, it will jump out. If you place it into a pot of room temperature water, then slowly increase the temperature to boiling, it will remain there and will die. My early self, the true innocent simple self, had been gradually and unnoticeably dying off most of my adult life, but what I lost back then was coming back to me now. I couldn't wait to rediscover that part of me and took every opportunity to do so.

My spending patterns were changing as well. My purchases were shifting from household, material goods to adventure gear and experience-related expenses. My personal relationships fell in line with this transition, as well. I began dating women in tune with simple living and the wonders of nature. I was coming full circle and loving it. Everything was richer, even though money was tighter than ever before. The quality of my intimate relationships, friendships, and family connections were all at a peak. I was playing hard and working hard in my business but still found my own unique balance point between work and life responsibilities, and that brought me contentment and a newfound happiness. Unlike riding a bike, however, balance in life requires constant intentional reflection and maintenance. Small, conscious course corrections. I was still asleep enough back then to drift off balance and began to pay the price.

Chapter 3 - JUST BREATHE

You know that feeling inside when you are about to do something stupid. Something out of alignment with who you really are deep inside, at your core. But you go ahead and do it anyway. It's one-part craving, one-part terror, and usually later on, one big part regret. Talk about sleepwalking. Around the end of 2002, my priorities began to change yet again. I was falling out of balance. I remember watching this train wreck from the outside, and thinking that it was someone else I was observing. I had run so low on cash that I needed to work a full-time job in addition to running my business. I was in a long-term relationship, which eventually led to marriage. This brought additional household duties into the mix, a relatively new thing for me. My mother was living nearby with a close family friend but I would often assist with her needs, as she was now in her mid-70's and living life alone without my dad. This left little time for cycling, adventuring and reflection, all serious food for my soul. I began eating on the road, often 3 meals a day. I recall many times chugging down a bacon, egg and cheese on a buttered bagel for breakfast, 3 slices of pizza for lunch, topped off with a cheeseburger or two and fries for dinner. Not nearly enough veggies, and fruit. Sometime none at all. I would eat so late at night that my full belly would keep me up for hours. Before I knew it, my alarm would go off at 6am and I'd start all over again. This self-imposed turbulence didn't end there. Without my daily connection to cycling and the natural world to keep me centered, grounded and recharged, I had amped up my social life to include late night pints and shots sometimes 5 nights a week, to help blow off steam. Dehydration was my normal mode of operation. I consumed very little water on a weekly basis, unless you count the water in the beer. I was burning my candle at both ends, along each side, then stepping on the damn thing in case the fire didn't do the trick. I was watching all this, but it just didn't click. I wasn't lazy or depressed, I was just clueless. Asleep at the wheel. It was like an out of body experience, that lasted years or like watching a TV rerun of a train wreck over and over, never getting tired of it, never changing the channel, until the channel is changed for you. The great mystery of all things has a way of telling us we are screwing up, and when it does, we're forced to listen. I don't remember my first Allergic Asthma incident. I do clearly remember the gradual, downward spiral leading up to the worst of it all. I was being deboned, dismantled, and dissolved in every way. The worst part of it was, I didn't really understand what was happening. The strangest things crossed my mind. Was I being punished for ignoring my mother's battle with Cancer, many years before? Would I have to go on disability like my dad had, after being injured on the job, when I was still a child? Would my girlfriend and housemate leave me because I lacked the energy and lung power to walk our dog? For anyone fortunate enough to have never experienced a breathing issue, here's what it's like, from my own unique viewpoint. I felt that every time I tried to inhale, the 10,000 lb. elephant sitting on my chest would step on my nostrils and shoot water down my throat with his trunk. Yes, a weird analogy, but for me accurate just the same. Getting out of bed to go pee in the morning felt like an Olympic event. My heart would race, in part from lack of oxygen but also from the panic induced by the feeling that I was drowning.

There are several different types of Asthma, caused by various factors, affecting millions of men, women and children each year. Most are thought to be caused by a blend of genetic and environmental factors. For me, my particular Asthma is called Allergic Asthma. My body reacts negatively to chemical vapors, pet dander, pollen and other influences such as dehydration and yes, poor diet. In some cases, particularly in children, stress is a significant factor. For me, I would come to discover that stress would actually alleviate my symptoms. For whatever reason, within my lungs, stress appears to indirectly offset the airway obstruction and inflammation most often associated with Asthma. Another type of Asthma, called Exercise-Induced Asthma which affects millions of athletes world-wide, would later complicate my own recovery.

During this difficult time, I spent more hours on the couch eating pretzels and feeling sorry for myself, than I care to remember. Within a relatively short period of time, I gained more than 20 pounds and was not exercising or even walking around outside at all. I stopped socializing with even my closest friends and I feared my significant other was giving up on me. That's when it really hit me. The icing on the cake. I may never improve. That's when depression became a factor. I remember the exact moment. That single point in time when I lost all hope, for the first time in my life. I was standing in my living room of the house we were renting at the time. It was a rural setting on a hazy autumn afternoon. Everything had a sepia tone to it. I looked out across the yard and thought about how difficult it was to simply walk out across the tree lined property. I remembered my bike trips out west and how strong I had been, at least most of the time. Riding over 10,000 foot Rocky Mountain passes, enjoying the camaraderie of close friends, while doing what I love to do. Testing and pushing myself outdoors in the natural world, with like-minded loved ones. Now, I'm looking out this window with shaky legs and a slight wheeze, feeling like I'm 100 years old. Probably looking like it, as well. My hands were cold and clammy, my shoulders were hunched and my new midsection stood out more than it should. I was in my mid-30s and already had elevated blood pressure and high cholesterol. What would be next...shit, am I going to die before even hitting 40?

During this time, I had been visiting doctors and allergists around my area. My primary care physician had put me on daily, long-term Asthma meds and prescribed me a rescue inhaler to carry, just in case of an attack. Attacks were usually not a major concern for me. My biggest problem was the consistent restriction and extreme fatigue. A lot of patients I spoke with at that time described their breathing as normal 95% of the time, then the other 5% was spent in a full blown Asthma attack. I had very few "attacks" but most every hour of every day was spent struggling for a decent breath. Imagine living your life feeling like you are drowning, slowly, all the time. It was unnerving, exhausting and discouraging. I would get angry at the world and think, the ability to breathe is everyone's God-given right. What the hell is going on here? This is bullshit. It's not fair, blah, blah and all that why me stuff came into play. I was missing the bigger picture. There was so much to see and learn.

I think when we're down and out, there's almost always a point when we say, enough is enough. If something doesn't break us entirely, we reach that point and stand back up with fight in our eyes and a spring in our step. For me, that came one morning in my upstairs bathroom. I was suffering the various side-effects of my medications. Most were developed to ease Asthma symptoms but, for me, they seemed to make things worse. I had a plastic bag full of these meds and I thought, I'm not doing everything that I can to help myself. First, I must control what I am able to control, then if that doesn't work, these meds have a place. But not before. I threw the bag under my sink, stepped over to my bed and began to formally reflect and meditate again for the very first time in several years. First, I took the time to fully absorb and accept my entire situation. Every little challenge and detail. I considered what part my own decisions had played into this mess. Why was I looking to the outside world for help with something, when I hadn't first looked inside? Then, there I was just sitting in the emptiness of the present moment. Observing. Without analysis. Without judgment. That was the beginning of a several week self-exploration. What came out of it couldn't have been simpler. A profound truth. Well, for me anyway. Slow down, open your eyes and follow your intuition...dumbass.

Leaning back into my project management and trouble-shooting background, I set out to organize the situation then take action toward a solution. Basically, a Game Plan and To Do list. I broke my life into chunks of stuff, in no particular order, based on what I felt made me tick and what I needed to focus on to improve my situation; water, food, exercise, rest, reflection, meditation, prayer, adventure, family, friends and business.

Next, I added ways I could improve each of these critical areas of my life. I looked for combo-efforts whenever possible. For example, cycling fed several areas at once – exercise, reflection, meditation, prayer, adventure, family and friends. That's how I reprioritized my world. Mindful reconstruction. Everything I chose to eat, drink or do had to be in alignment with my Allergic Asthma recovery game plan. My top goals were getting off all meds and getting back outside riding my bike. I knew feeling good would be a natural outcome of achieving those two goals so I didn't want to overthink it. I didn't need to. I tried to keep things as simple as possible. The simpler the approach, the greater the chances of pulling it off, I thought.

Enjoying my friends over drinks at the bar still fit but on my terms and in alignment with my Asthma Management efforts and overall health and wellness Game Plan. I'd avoid the chicken wings and choose lighter, less hoppy beers. Intense hops tended to aggravate my symptoms. I'd avoid environmental triggers like cigarette smoke and perfume and get home in time to get a good night's sleep. Not much of a sacrifice really. I was getting back into balance. Rediscovering, maybe even finding for the very first time, my own unique balance point. Sure, I would stray once in a while but as long as I took the time to reflect on what I was doing wrong, I found I could easily correct my course. As long as I wasn't asleep at the wheel, I could see and address a not-so-wise choice before it left behind a long, unmanageable debris trail. A trail that would trip up both myself and sometimes others around me. I revisited my personal relationships and began focusing more on quality then quantity, and followed the same practice with my business, in every waking hour.

One by one, I continued to consciously address each of my critical areas of focus. I was now drinking 6 to 8 glasses of water daily. I shifted my food intake from ultra-processed road-trip specials to organic lean meats, fruits and vegetables, as often as possible. I made an effort to eat my last meal of the day earlier, to improve digestion. I began taking supplements geared toward respiratory and cardiovascular health. I set aside a small chunk of time each day for deep reflection, meditation and prayer. This fed a subtler side of me, that was always there but few people in my life (including myself) had ever seen. I was gaining a higher perspective and both the ups and downs in my life were finding a comfortable home within my head and heart.

Now mind you, I wasn't neurotic about any of this. This was a long journey and I tripped up along the way, many times, and I still do. But each time, I tried my best to rise to the challenge and continue on, experiencing many teachings in the process. Some I applied to business and some back into my own personal life. Sometimes, both. I kept this entire journey from most of my friends, even the closest, at times. When it came to my newfound life challenges/obstacles, I didn't want to be a burden so I would disappear for weeks at a time, and not call anyone or hang out. They had their own problems and I didn't want to add mine into the mix. Besides, I needed the down time. Just me, my then fiancé and my mom. I must have been a handful during this time, and I thank them for their patience, love and support each step of the way.

The only two key areas in my life that were still sketchy were exercise and adventure. I was gradually breathing easier, I was losing the weight I had gained, and my endurance was improving, but I still lacked the conditioning and confidence to go out for a bike ride. I was able to do moderate household chores, aside from changing the kitty litter and brushing our dog Angus. These chores were huge triggers. The ability to do anything physical felt terrific. I never thought I'd get excited about moving around the house, tidying up and knocking out domestic To Do lists. This was never my thing. I was out walking short distances and even completed light hikes solo and with friends, but I couldn't get my head around cycling. I had a strong, underlying fear of suffering an Allergic Asthma incident somewhere out in the woods or along a quiet country road. I would see myself gasping and crashing into a roadside ditch, passing out and dying before any help could be summoned. The part of my ego that fueled my fearlessness and wanderlust had been dented in a big way. I went from bulletproof to ultra-cautious. Eventually, I pulled myself together and pulled out one of my mountain bikes. I could no longer resist. It had sat for so long, unridden, the frame was now coated with a thick layer of dirty dust and the chain was rusty and stiff, along with the well-worn brake and shifter cables. I pulled out my bicycle tools, equally dusty and began tuning my once formidable steed. Well, that didn't go very well. Bending up and down combined with turning wrenches and inhaling Teflon spray lube kicked my lungs in the groin. I had to lay down for 2 hours and eventually lost interest in my restoration project.

Two weeks later, I tried again. This time I sat on a stool, to minimize the ups and downs and wore a painter's mask to avoid sucking down any oily mist. I paced myself, which would prove to be my new MO, and finished the tune-up in time for a quick ride at dusk. I made it up and down the drive-way...once. That didn't go so well either. I can't recall whether I had an Asthma attack or a panic attack, but either way I felt I should have been wearing a little baby blue secu-rity blanket instead of a fancy bicycle jersey.

Each day I'd go out and ride a little longer, up and down the driveway. I would focus on my breathing and pedaling to keep my exertion at a reasonable level. The process was te-dious but it felt so good to be back in the saddle and self-propelled. Of course, it wasn't all good. How can I put this delicately? My ass hurt big time. I had forgotten how painful it was for a cyclist to jump on a bike and ride for the first time in many months. After a break from riding, your tender body forgets what it's like to have something so unnatural pressed into its sit bones and soft tissue. There is no feeling quite so uncomfortable.

After several days, I included our main road in my daily rou-tine, slowly progressing to a local rail trail. Just seeing and feeling the trees again gave me a huge boost. I felt like I had thrust forward years in days, just by breathing in nature and feeling the mud pop up and pepper my shins. It was extraor-dinary. My next step was to head back out to my old stomping grounds at Minnewaska State Park. I always felt there was something magical about those cliffside trails. I still do. I can still remember those first few rides out there, after my return to the saddle. I did a lot of hill walking. I even had to walk down some of the steep hills to keep my breathing under control. I also recall returning with my friends. We would all go out on a Saturday or Sunday morning, in a big group of mixed riders. Some, much more confident and accomplished than others. We'd call it a "family ride" to indicate we were not in hardcore mode and that it was okay to relax and fall behind. No pressure. Years before I spent a lot of time at the front, darting up and down the narrow rocky trails, uninterested in the 80-foot drop below. Now I found myself bringing up the rear with new or light recreational cyclists. At first it was twisting and turning my ego a bit. I had to wrestle with that awhile but soon settled into my place at the back of the pack, ensuring everyone was safe and mechanically supported. Eventually, I grew to enjoy that role and continued it on future rides even after my endurance had improved.

When I look back, it's clear that breathing was always somewhat of an issue growing up and into adulthood. There were times running in gym class, playing floor hockey and other school sports when I would get easily winded. I was never particularly thin and athletic so I assumed it was just an unwanted by-product of second helpings and my remarkably deformed flat feet and collapsing ankles. I once had a well-known Orthopedic surgeon, who typically treated professional athletes, tell me that I had the flattest feet and weakest ankles he had ever seen and that I shouldn't be able to play hockey, bicycle, go backpacking or even walk properly for that matter. I left his office and never went back. It's up to me to determine what I can and cannot do, I thought. To this day, I try to keep that notion fresh in my mind.

I can now recognize how my Allergic Asthma played into one pre-diagnosis bike trip out west, around 2003. I was backcountry touring with 3 other close friends. We were riding the Colorado section of the multi-state, 2,745 mile Great Divide Mountain Bike Trail. It was a 300+ mile leg, in total, consisting of long days, and some serious elevation gains and high altitude passes. I was hanging in there but began to struggle on several, long uphill sections. Out west, in high peaks country, it is not uncommon to ride up steep hills for hours at a time. When touring, the extra outdoor gear adds to the challenge. At one point, after riding uphill for what seemed forever, my teammates pulled ahead and arrived at the top of Indiana Pass, the highest point along the entire GDMBR, elevation 11,910 feet. My heart rate soared, and I struggled, gasping for breath, beyond anything I had ever experienced. I knew I was in big trouble. When I finally reached the top, my crew was already done relaxing and ready to continue. I was last again, as I had been so many times in childhood. I fell back onto the ground. I knew at that moment something was seriously wrong with my body. I was having an Asthma incident before I even knew what that was or felt like. Something serious enough that my will and conditioning might not win out. Translation: No matter how prepared, stupid or stubborn I was, there in that moment in the middle of nowhere, I could die. I thought of giving up at that point, and several times again, during that same trip. I didn't discuss it with anyone. Again, I didn't want to be a burden. Everyone was out there for a reason or combination of reasons. Mostly it was for the pure adventure of it all. I didn't want to kill their buzz and I knew I needed to be out there too. I needed to explore and experience nature, firsthand with these special friends, while stretching myself and my rig along the way.

Being out there, riding long days, can be extreme but peaceful and rejuvenating at the same time, if that makes any sense. I suppose it depends on the type of person you are and what peaks your interest at that particular point in your life. I think there's a place for armchair adventures, as well. They can serve a purpose, beyond simple entertainment. They can spark you up and get you moving. Studying other more accomplished adventurers helps educate you on what destinations may interest you the most and how to plan for the experience most efficiently. For me, reading about talented, free-spirited climbers and mountaineers like Yvon Chouinard, Lynn Hill, Ed Viesturs, and Reinhold Messner had always done the trick. It both inspired and motivated me to stretch into the unknown. A place that most of us fear, while others seek it out, embrace it, and cannot get enough of it.

Something changes in us when we push into and through our fears. The result can be personal growth beyond our wildest imagination. True survival stories, such as *Touching the Void*, help illustrate our primal adventure spirit combined with our relentless will to live. Stories such as this fueled my fire from a young age and would later keep me company on long, solo nights on the trail bikepacking or in the woods hiking and camping. On nights when my lungs closed up and fear crept in, I would recall those learned lessons of strength, wisdom, courage, respect and personal growth. They permeated my past and would help mold my future.

Around the time of my official Allergic Asthma diagnosis and return to cycling, I began exploring different cycling styles and equipment. I had many years of experience building, tuning and repairing all types of bicycles and had most all of the special tools needed to configure any rig I wished to test out. I was desperate to come up with something that would be fun to ride and easier on my heart and lungs than a traditional bike. It needed to be trail-friendly and have lots of low, hill climbing gears. Perhaps the obvious choice was not a big, heavy, rear-suspended long wheelbase recumbent, but that's what I chose to build up just the same. Instinctively it just felt right....at the time. I knew I'd catch a lot of ribbing from my riding buddies but if this configuration helped me breathe better and keep up with them, they'd get over it. Well, in hindsight, that didn't really go as planned.

I built up this Burley brand, recumbent bicycle around the winter of 2004. It was originally designed for road use and light touring. The riding position was stretched out and laid back and the cockpit looked and felt more like a chopper motorcycle than a bicycle. The handlebars were raised and the seat hung down low. At first, handling proved to be a challenge. I had to learn how to ride all over again. On a traditional bicycle, you can use your body to steer in an intuitive, automatic way. On an upright, long wheelbase recumbent, the action and effect of leaning is a bit different. To this day, I can't quite describe in what way it's different but as a cyclist you just know. In any case, this was one comfy ride. Like riding your Lazy Boy downhill all day. In fact, it was so easy, I soon got bored and started thinking up more challenging terrain and new day rides.

During this time, my breathing was still bad but my rescue inhaler helped maintain my false sense of security and my gradual weight loss and new upright position raised my confidence level a notch. This shot-in-the-arm aligned with my circle of close adventure cyclist buddies chatting up another bike trip out west. This time it would be the Montana section of the Great Divide Mountain Bike Route and I was in. Initially, they had no idea what I had been training on or exactly why. I was still fairly private about my breathing issues and the word "recumbent" was not even in their vocabulary. This was going to be good, I thought. I remember the moment I first mentioned I had built up a recumbent and I was planning to use it for this 7+ day off-road adventure through some of the most technically challenging sections of the entire GDMBR. There was some curiosity at first followed by light skepticism, then closed out with outright disbelief. They are talented and knowledgeable athletes all with extensive back-country experience, on and off mountain bikes, but this was uncharted territory. I was seriously questioning my decision to go through with this, on any bike. I flip-flopped, privately, for many days and weeks even after committing. In the end, my (and their) common sense went out the window and it remained a go. I was about to do something that few, if any had ever done successfully. Tour a full section of the GDMBR on a semi-loaded recumbent. What the hell was I thinking? Thinking had nothing to do with it.

Once the final decision was made, I jumped in with both feet. I kicked up my physical and mental training and Asthma Management education and skills, and began rebuilding my recumbent. Riding this 40 lb. steel easy chair up monster Montana hills, on loose dirt and rocks, would be very differ-ent than cruising my local, relatively level, paved running paths. I started with beefing up my wheelset. Thicker spokes, puncture-resistant inner tubes and wide off-road tires were a must. Next, this roadie drivetrain needed a mountain-minded overhaul. I added lower gears to tackle the signifi-cant daily elevation gain and extra wide mountain bike pedals and flat off-road handlebars for improved handling. I replaced all the internal bearings and spindles with off-road worthy versions, in anticipation of the substantial forces required to move the bike, my own body weight, plus another 45 lbs. of camping gear and tools. Lastly, I added a rear rack and panniers and a special recumbent-friendly seat pack that mounted directly behind me. I was ready. Well, not quite.

During training I had several breathing issues that sometimes sidetracked me for days. Something I hadn't quite expected. My riding position was so good for my breathing that I began to push myself too hard and my heart would beat too fast, for too long. If this aligned with the right combination of allergy triggers, I would experience a breathing "incident." It was Allergic Asthma meets Exercise-Induced Asthma, resulting in sheer terror followed by exhaustion, capped off by a burning desire to say, "Screw it, I'm done. Back to the couch." It was then I decided to religiously train and trip with a heart rate monitor (HRM), and log my data for post-training review. I had some experience with athletic HRMs already so this was a natural fit. It was a little added work upfront and after, but the payoff came during the ride. I was able to carefully regulate my heart rate within a safe range. For me, at that time, my magic number was somewhere between 113 and 126 beats-per-minute (BPM). I knew that if I was above the 113, I was working hard enough to manage my weight and maintain my fitness and if I remained below the 126, I would not induce any Asthma symptoms. Later, I used the Internet to share my training and bike trip heart rate data with other athletes suffering from breathing issues. Some found it useful, most found it encouraging at the very least.

After months of preparation and training, it was time for one last doctor's appointment. Once I had the green light from my doctor, I was home free. I was sure with all my hard work, all would go very well. I was wrong. For anyone with a breathing-related condition, the thought of breathing into a Peak Flow Meter brings with it mixed emotions. For me, at first, I saw it as a challenge. An opportunity for a new personal best. Here's how it goes. You breathe in and fill your lungs to maximum capacity. Then you push that lung-full of air as violently as possible into this little device. The incoming air pushes up an indicator. You then repeat this test 3 times in a row, unless of course you pass out in the process. The doc takes the best of 3. After my initial diagnosis about a year before, I was blowing less than 400 which is not good at all. Since then, it began to slowly improve. This time I was certain I would break the 650 mark. When I fell in well under 520, I was devastated. Here I was, committed to my most challenging event yet, and I was blowing relatively weak numbers. These numbers along with long, steep ascents in thin, mountainous air would increase the risk factor 10 fold. Once again, I had serious doubts about doing this. My family was against it, my doctor was against it, and my common sense was telling me to stay local and play on flat, paved paths followed by afternoon siestas in my backyard hammock.

I remember thinking, what if I keel over on this trip? My last moments would be spent on a bicycle that looks a lot like a muddy lawn chair on wheels. Then I thought about how far I had come since my diagnosis. I remembered how beautiful the clear western night sky could be. How dewy and crisp the morning air was and how spending time with good friends in isolated regions can be medicine in itself. I recalled an elevating 7 day, southwestern states, Four Corners adventure with my very special friend Patty, years before, that continues to inspire me to this day. I needed this and I would remain committed to complete it or collapse trying and I appeared to be ok with that. Not a bad way to meet your end, I thought. I've always believed that if you leave this physical world doing what you truly love, for all the right reasons, there is no reason for fear and there should be no regrets. Well, it's easy to say that, but once you're in deep, things get complicated. Moment-to-moment battles with doubt and fear present themselves when you least expect them to. Sometimes at the worst times and on any trip such as this, but doubt and fear can be more dangerous than the undertaking itself.

We had decided to ship our bicycles out west to Montana, ahead of us, to a bike shop local to our starting point. I can still hear the shop owner's voice asking which one of us is the stupid one. This shop had been regularly hosting Great Divide riders for years and not once had they heard of anyone attempting this Montana section on a recumbent of any kind. As he plainly put it, "I doubt it's ever been done and I'm pretty sure I'll see you back here very soon, without your friends." That rang in my ears the entire time we bought supplies and staged our gear at our rental cabin before heading out on day-one. My friends' first impressions of my loaded rig added to my angst. None were comfortable balancing it, two said I was absolutely nuts to attempt this, and one almost crashed it into a hedge. Not a good sign.

Riding out on that first morning, I reflected on everything that had happened in my life over the past 5 years. All the ups and every down. I thought about my reasons for going forward with this challenge. Years ago my motivation would have been completely different. Before losing my father and before my Asthma diagnosis, I would be here only for the rush, the bragging rights, flirting with the local ladies, and the booze. I had since experienced a slight but lasting glimpse of something bigger than...me. I was now here more for the pure experience of it all. Action without an agenda, without image. Well not exactly, as my friends would attest to, but heading that way at least.

I think many people go through these same mini-awakenings naturally as they grow older, start families and care for aging parents. Many of us though fail to recognize this and the importance of it all. My growing practice of intense, deep reflection on this entire process exposed a new world to me. A world some may call, divine. For me, it was becoming clear that God, love, cosmic balance, creativity and ultimate truth were always one and always there but it's tough to see that when your vision is cloudy. When your heart is distracted and your mind is diluted. This trip was the next step for me. One step closer to a second half of life awareness and conscious living. My next little glimpse at the truth of it all and I was ready.

Things started off well. We were riding in a tight formation, chatting and laughing along the way. The hills were as difficult as I had anticipated but the elevation gains combined with trail dust soon presented an unexpected challenge. Dirt that goes airborne, over high mountain passes, is bad news for anyone with Asthma under any circumstances. I tried to cover my mouth and breathe through a bandana, and even a spare sock on occasion, but there were moments when puffs and chunks made it through to my mouth and throat, eventually settling in my lungs. I knew my rescue inhaler was only inches from my grip, however, reaching for it while piloting this bizarre, awkward, laid-back bicycle would surely result in a face plant or I suppose an ass plant would be a better choice of words given that my bouncing bottom sat about 8" from the hard pack trail surface. Hours of that degree of exposure were taking their toll. Good conversation helped distract me but, at times, it was a chore to ward off the constant fear of losing my breath and launching out of control. I started to use a simple meditation-in-motion as a tool to keep myself together. I would simply observe my breath aligning with my pedal strokes and focus on the fullness of each. This would help slow my heart rate and at times regulate my breathing through the harsh trail conditions.

This trip in total was going to fall in around 500 miles and would eventually take us 10 days to complete. We averaged 50 miles a day in the saddle with some sessions peaking at over 70 miles. Several days in, stopped for the night at a small cottage. After we ate, and talked about the challenges of the long day of riding we had just put behind us, we each picked a corner of the room to crash in. With sleeping bags in hand, we hobbled off in different directions. That was a long night for me. I couldn't sleep. I laid there most of the night thinking about quitting, for my own sake and for the sake of my team-mates. My heart was racing and my breathing was seriously labored. I had taken a few meds but had to be careful to not impact my next day's riding with unwanted side effects. It was an ongoing balance between prevention and treatment. A very delicate balance. I wish I could have balanced that as successfully as balancing a bicycle but it never came easy. There were always curve balls. Like the morning I took too much decongestant for irritated and painful sinuses. It jacked me up so bad that my heart rate soared and actually trig-gered my symptoms.

That next morning was rainy and cool, with the sun peek-ing out through the haze. A beautifully typical Montana sunrise. I was weak, wheezing a bit, had a brutal headache but couldn't imagine being anywhere else doing anything else at that very moment. This was the foulest, best medicine in the world for me and I loved it all.

As the days went on, I began to physically suffer in ways I had never quite experienced before. Halfway through the trip, my legs felt like burning concrete blocks. On this bike I could not easily shift my riding position, so my legs, back, neck and shoulders all began to stiffen and ache. Later on, pain would come with a sharp intensity. I've always considered myself someone with a good tolerance for pain, but this trip caused me to reconsider that image of myself.

Now, in addition to breathing through what seemed like a dirty, wet, paper bag for 11 hours at a time, I could no longer trust my legs to propel me at a suitable pace. My second worst-case scenario was becoming real. I was falling behind and my team was paying the price. After riding up steep hills for several hours, they would sit waiting for me to catch up. At times they were more than 30 minutes ahead of me. By the time I arrived, I had no opportunity to stop and rest. As a courtesy to them and tribute to their patience, I would continue on without pause, grimacing with every pedal stroke. Eventually it became a joke. I think the humor helped me cope. I think it helped them cope as well. The humor didn't end there. At one point, through Grizzly country near Polebridge, Montana, my caring and compassionate pack joked about stuffing my panniers with salmon as I brought up the rear, alone, while they road up ahead. Their logic was sound. We had heard that Glacier National Park often relocated their aggressive Grizzlies to this isolated area and, of course, predators always stalk the slowest and weakest of any pack. I would have been laughing too, if I wasn't the one trailing behind.

The trail conditions were beginning to worsen and I was drifting back and flailing more and more with every mile. Loose dust turned into soft, rocky, double and single track. Fallen trees and thick brush added to our obstacles. It was then when I experienced the worst and best elements of this adventure challenge. I had hit bottom physically but even worse, I lost my mental/emotional edge. Anyone will tell you, rides like this test you physically but your mental state is far more important to your overall success. In fact, for me, it's always been about 70% mental/30% physical. In the midst of this train wreck, my teammates began unpacking my gear and redistributing it amongst their bikes. I didn't have to ask and I didn't have words to express my appreciation. Here I am, rolling behind like a big ball and chain for days. They should have left me at one of our overnight stops. They could have, but they didn't. Not only did they keep me around, they were now shouldering my weight for me. On the surface, I could not believe this but deep down it didn't surprise me. These are not just friends. They are family. These are only some of the extraordinary people who were there for my mother and me, when we lost my father in 2000. A life-changing time. We may not all see each other every day, but my loyalty and gratitude will never diminish. This gesture was truly the most important part of my entire Montana Great Divide experience. A pride-dinger for me for sure, but a great lesson in teamwork, loyalty and friendship. Many thanks to Bob, Kathy and Jim for their kindness and hard work.

The GDMBR, at that time, was about 2,500 miles long and ran down the U.S. north to south from Canada to Mexico. We were about to experience the most aggressive downhill section of this entire route. It was steep, technical, grassy and I was about to do it on a semi-loaded long wheelbase recumbent. Very exciting, in a bizarre sort of way. It was sketchy but all 4 of us made it down safely. I was in a great headspace and earned enough adrenaline and trail credibility to make it through the day strong, with my self-esteem intact.

Overall, the Montana trip was a success but it wasn't without its difficulties and several long-term problems. My output had been much higher than expected. My heart rate monitor calculated that I had burned 42,000 kcal during that 10-day period. I hadn't taken in enough calories to cover what I was burning along the way. Same goes for water. Electrolyte levels were a constant issue. I ran on the edge of dehydration the entire time. I burned fat but also lost muscle mass, which I hadn't expected. In total, I lost about 10 lbs. Also, my average daily heart rate of 145 beats-per-minute (BPM) was considerably higher than my trip target range of 113 to 126 BPM. This certainly contributed to my exhaustion and occasionally affected my blood sugar levels but most importantly it impacted my breathing. By day's end, I would often experience a rapid heart rate, high anxiety, and the beginning signs of Exercise-Induced Asthma, a serious, secondary concern of mine from the very beginning of this adventure. I used informal meditation techniques to help lower my heart rate and aid in my overall recovery.

On the upside, I was formally tracking, noting and later analyzing all my riding data, as it related to my Allergic Asthma. After a while, it became a fun diversion. The information I had compiled, helped me train for future trips in a safe and highly effective manner. I even began sharing my data with other athletes interested in managing their Asthma, for peak performance.

As previously mentioned, trail dust became an unpleasant highlight of that trip. Loose clay-like dirt would settle on forest road surfaces until kicked up by passing 4x4s and logging trucks. Over time, I felt as if this dirt-dust was packing into my nasal passages, sinus cavities and lungs. How much of that feeling was real and how much was amplified by my growing fear of having an Asthma incident out in the middle of nowhere, I can't say for sure. That's one of those tricky Asthma things some of us battle with. Is it real or imagined? Can I work through it...safely, or am I putting myself at great risk if I continue? Keep going or slow down or stop completely? When in doubt, I keep going. I find that 80% of the time, it's the fear of what can happen making me feel worse than I really am. Once I face and embrace that fear, I begin to feel better. Healthier. Stronger. That's not to say I don't slow down, take inventory and make small adjustments. That's part of responsible Asthma Management. But once I do, I go on, with as much confidence as I can muster.

If you can imagine doing thousands of leg presses at the gym, for 9+ hours a day, 10 days in a row, you begin to understand what it was like pedaling a loaded recumbent up huge hills across an entire state, throughout that trip. At the start, the reclined riding position was my friend. I was relaxed and could see scenery that I had often missed while touring on traditional mountain bikes. At first I actually felt guilty that I had it so easy, while my riding partners were tortured by their hard, narrow seats for hours on end. But then, my friendly riding position became my worst nightmare. Several days into the trip, I was building up lactic acid in my quads from grinding up those big hills. Recumbents do not allow for much adjustment in positioning, while riding. You're pretty much stuck with leaning backward against a web seat and seatback, while your legs are stretched out forward, suspended, while pedaling one rotation after another, for hours and hours. Stopping was never really an option, since I had mentally committed to keeping up with my team mates on their traditional bikes. When they became uncomfortable, they could always stand, shift their weight from side to side, or stretch out their back while coasting down a hill. For me, this was never an option. A much needed mid-trip medical massage, near Columbia Falls, MT helped to break up the lactic acid and get me back onto the trail.

The after-effect of this high-force, repetitive motion was foot, leg and hip pain that lingered for many months following my return home, but a chronic lower back pain was the real sleeper. It wasn't debilitating but it was always there to some degree. Later, a doctor would suggest I had a disk issue. He was sure that my laid back riding position, in combination with the extreme nature of our Montana event, was the root cause. The word surgery was mentioned but when it comes to back issues, I'll opt for rest and stretches every time. I had to cancel several bike trips, but my approach paid off and within 2 years, I was fully healed. It was during this period that I began experimenting with my standing position, riding seatless. Not only was this new position helping me with my breathing issues, it was more comfortable for my lower back. I believe it helped to stretch and strengthen my abs and lower back muscles. It was becoming clear that cycling standing up would become a big part of my future.

Chapter 4 - THE STANDING CYCLIST

I returned home from Montana in early August, 2005. I had overtaxed my system and was now paying the price. My body hurt from head to toe. I was weak, jet lagged and had a sinus infection and a head cold which spread down into my chest. This of course can mean big trouble for Asthma sufferers or anyone with breathing challenges. Upper respiratory issues can get real ugly, real quick. Doped up on cold and flu meds and antibiotics, I drifted around my house bouncing between my bed and a living room futon for almost two weeks and took the next 2 months off, from training, to recover from our tour. I needed every single one of those recovery days.

I did a lot of thinking during that time and had some ups and downs. I couldn't believe how bad I felt and how long it took me to bounce back. Sure, this trip was hard but it shouldn't have affected me to this extent. Should it have? I mean after all, I do have Asthma, right? But, so what? But, I have Asthma, I thought. Back and forth. Life is full of cross-roads and for me that was one of them. I was stuck standing right at the center for many weeks. I stood there and thought, "I am seriously limited. I never thought I was, but now I do. Should I be questioning my ability to cycle and ad-venture tour? Can I ever live a truly normal life?" I wrestled with these thoughts of limitation, day and night. I would go out, see friends, party a bit and try to forget it all for a while, but those nagging doubts would come bursting back into my head, and all bets were off.

Somewhere in there, was yet another defining moment. I can't recall exactly when it was or where I was at the time. Perhaps it was during some sleepless night worrying about my business or my recent marriage. Maybe I was out hiking or tinkering with one of my bikes. Somewhere in there I had decided to take it one breath at a time. One mile at a time. To lighten up, pace my second bounce back, and fully enjoy the process. I began to reflect on the last several years. I started out denying my Asthma. Later, in Montana, I was out to fight it and prove something even if it killed me. Well it almost did. Or at least it felt that way. Now, the theme for me would be freedom. Freedom from any storyline and judgment of myself or my circumstances. The truth was what is was, nothing more, nothing less. This time, I had to accept my challenges while still finding all the best ways to work through all obstacles. I had to redefine my expectations and redesign the experience of riding, touring, traveling and performing with Allergic Asthma. I thought, who knows, maybe I'll even enjoy this. Yes, this Asthma was a limitation, to some degree, but that didn't mean that I was limited. I am not this condition, it's just something that my body experiences. It's not who I am. I may have Asthma, I thought, but whether or not I call myself an Asthmatic is entirely up to me. Time to, once again, roll forward.

It didn't take long for me to sketch out bicycle designs that might improve my ability to ride with both a breathing issue and a simmering lower back injury. At first, nothing worked on paper. The body positions didn't play out. My wife at the time was a Physical Educator and many of my close friends were seasoned athletes. Most weighed in on the subject including one very talented Exercise Physiologist, Trainer and Wellness Coach. Kim is a longtime friend who would later become my most trusted and valued partner and resource in my Standing Cyclist endeavors as well as daily life. An expert in biomechanics, she would teach me many things that would help propel me and my machines forward in the years to come.

The bulk of my own design concepts were rightfully slammed by this reputable group. Too rough on the ankles, too steep of an angle for the knees, too much stress on the hands and wrists. Sore neck, pulled muscles, the list went on and on. I decided to prototype some bikes using the hundreds of spare bicycle parts I had accumulated over the years. I built and rebuilt version after version, measuring tube lengths and angles and tested many riding configurations along the way. I began to notice the comfort of one particular riding position. I was getting somewhere, however, my back was upright. Almost totally vertical, but not quite. It allowed my diaphragm to fully open when inhaling, to maximize my breath. It was also comfortable for my lower back, as long as I didn't drift too close to fully upright, at which point I'd experience issues, usually in the form of lower back twinges. That wouldn't do. I needed to limit the extension of my back while still remaining close enough to the handlebars to maintain control at higher speeds and when cornering.

After about a month of trial and error, I found what I believed to be the perfect position. One catch. It took me up off of my saddle. Completely off, the entire time. I'd be riding this thing standing up. The final formula, at that time, was to raise the cockpit (handlebars/stem) by installing new front forks with an uncut steerer tube. This allows the stem and bars to be mounted much higher than normally possible without compromising handling. I chose a fork with a steel steerer tube to maximize strength for safety reasons. I used an extra wide, extra tall, BMX racing handlebar mounted to a thick BMX stem. All angles were chosen carefully to provide the perfect position for my particular body geometry.

Experienced cyclists know that shifting gears while standing is often a dangerous and unpredictable action. To avoid this issue, and to help keep things as simple as possible, I chose a 32x18 single-speed setup. One gear, no shifting required. I tried out several different frames, for my final configuration, but none fit my overall concept as well as an old San Andreas downhill mountain bike frame I had laying around. It was perfect for several reasons. All the tube angles were correct, it was beefy to withstand the added, constant force resulting from my new standing style, and best of all, it had a fully removable seat tube assembly. This meant that I would have plenty of open space below my bottom in case of a slip up while riding. No seat, no seat post and now no seat tube at all. Nothing but air. To get the perfect head tube angle, for the best handling while riding in this upright position, I ran a slightly larger 29er wheel/tire upfront with a 26" wheel/tire in the rear. This gave me the exact road feel I was looking for. Large downhill racing platform pedals, one brake and a front handlebar bag rounded off the package.

Now that I had settled on a bike setup, I needed to begin training on it. I needed to figure out the best way to ride this thing and ride it far. On-road, off-road, whatever came my way. I knew that maintaining a proper riding position, for any cyclist, is critical for performance and to prevent injury. What I was starting with here broke all the rules. Was this a recipe for disaster? One of cycling's golden rules is to stand less and sit more. Sitting uses less energy. When sitting, you're fully leveraging the mechanical advantage you gain from riding versus, let's say running, for example. So, was this more like running than riding?

Another big no-no is riding with your knees too far forward. This increases the stress on your knees and over time can cause serious injury. When you ride standing on a traditional bike, often clipped into the pedals for added riding efficiency, your knees drift forward. That's another good reason why cyclists minimize their time out of the saddle. So, am I way off base here, I thought. Possibly, but I decided to let my body decide. I formalized a training routine, at first riding on a magnetic resistance trainer in my basement during the winter months. On light snow days, I would train on the road in my rural Pennsylvania community. I was learning how to ride a bike all over again. I found, over time, that I was developing an instinct for where my feet needed to be, on the pedals. Too far forward, I would get lower knee pain. Too far back on the pedals and I would blow up my calf muscles. My elbows needed to be slightly bent to keep a soft, suspended feel on the bike. That was also my way of keeping my back at the right angle. Upon measurement, I later found that angle to land around 70 degrees. Frequent in-motion changes in position allowed me to ride comfortably, in the beginning, for almost one hour without stopping. Of course cadence, or pedal rotations per minute, was an important focus with regards to my Asthma. I found that with the gearing I had chosen, I could stay within my anti-Asthma target zone, when spinning at about 60 RPM. Not much, but then again, not many people ride standing up for more than a couple minutes at a time, so I was encouraged.

My heart rate monitor and my personal wellness checkpoints became key components in my training. I trained 95% of the time with my monitor to avoid Asthma issues and tracked and analyzed my progress each day and again each month. My wellness checkpoints helped me stay in balance, both in my training and in my personal and professional life. I logged everything from food intake, to hydration, to bowel movements and even my pH levels (saliva and urine) to ensure proper digestion. I tracked supplements taken, moods experienced, sleep patterns, my spiritual practice, and the quality of my relationships. Everything plays a part in good health and athletic performance. That's something I learned early on, when struggling to get back up and outside years before. To this day, my trip training routine remains much the same.

PART TWO

Chapter 5 - IRELAND

Now that the bike and my training were coming along, I was getting restless. I needed a goal. A trip. An adventure. Not just any adventure but something worthy of all my effort and progress. Something that would trump Montana but would hopefully not end me in the process. My breathing was strong. I was med-free and my back was much improved although still not perfect. My stand-up training had allowed me to rest the muscles that needed resting while stretching out and strengthening the rest. I needed to really push myself and test my limits. Not to prove something, like in Montana, but to exercise the freedom I had earned through design (the bike), balance (my life) and plain old hard work and persistence. I needed to get away from everyone and everything and really put myself out on a limb. I had considered a solo trip out west but I had already logged many miles in the Rockies. The bike-friendly country of Denmark deserved some research and soon worked its way up on my shortlist but, for whatever reason, I just couldn't commit.

Life has a way of shuffling and aligning our puzzle pieces in meaningful ways, bringing together the right mix of options and catalysts, at just the right time. For me Sinead, a soul-friend of mine or Anam Cara in the Celtic tradition, was one such catalyst who led me down an important road. A path to The Emerald Isle. Originally from Ireland, Sinead was introduced to me by Laura, another great soul-friend in my life, many seasons before. Now years later, Sinead would become my expert in all things Irish. It was her snappy brogue, energy and encouragement that sealed my deal. I made the decision to take this standing cyclist show on the road, to Ireland. My "plan" was to plan as little as possible. This would be a quest and a pilgrimage of sorts. The trip theme became an exciting combination of freedom, spontaneity, and adventure within the context of reaching beyond my preconceived boundaries. Don't get me wrong, I did my homework, bought my maps, and packed my bike tools and a spare rescue inhaler, but beyond that, my fate was in the hands of the universe, a higher power, ascended masters...and of course the directionally challenged tourists driving their rental cars on the wrong side of the road.

As it turned out, the adventure began before even leaving the states. Thunderstorms and flash flooding contributed to heavy traffic along the New York State Thruway, my primary route towards Newark Airport. I planned on leaving my car up north and taking a shuttle bus down to the airport, but I missed not one but two bus departures and found myself driving all the way down to Newark from PA. Arriving late, I hurried through the wet and windy airport economy parking lot dragging two gear bags and a big cardboard box stuffed with pieces that only the night before resembled a bright red and black circus bike. The wetter the cardboard box got, the weaker it got. I wondered if I'd even make it to the ticket counter before it totally disintegrated. I began to panic, imagining myself juggling handlebars and crank arms at the ticket counter, while fumbling around for my soggy ID.

The flight was a red eye that would dump me out at Shannon Airport in southwest Ireland the following morning. Excited about my upcoming adventure, I didn't get much sleep. I did chat with an elderly couple returning from a cruise. When I explained what I intended to do, they laughed thinking I was a jokester. I didn't try to convince them otherwise. Perhaps they were right. For a moment, I thought, maybe this really was just a big joke.

Upon arrival, sometime around 6:30am Ireland time, I retrieved my awkward bike box from the oversized baggage claim area, unpacked my small tool kit and began building my seatless, single-speed touring bike in the middle of the airport lobby. I stashed the empty bike box in an airport locker, for reuse upon my return. My riding gear fit into two bags. I carried energy bars, one inhaler, and my maps in a small handlebar bag. I traveled with two sets of clothes. One set I wore and the extra set travelled along on my back in an ultralight day pack which also contained first aid supplies, bike tools, a couple of spare parts, a head lamp for late night riding and my backup inhaler. Time to head out. But to where? That was the beauty of this trip. I would decide each day's route, that morning or the night before. At times I would simply follow the "signs". People I met along the way might mention something interesting and this would nudge me in a particular direction. I soon dubbed this approach The Adventure Way. Family members would later highlight similarities between myself and my Grandfather Angelo and Great Uncle Al who, early in the 1900s, hoboed across the U.S. seeking adventure. It's a reputation I carry with me happily to this day.

I started out riding on N19 which led me away from the airport. This was a busy road filled with distracted vacationers attempting to decipher road signs and navigate fast-paced traffic circles, called roundabouts. All this, while trying to avoid hitting me or best case running me off the road. I felt like that little steel ball in a pinball machine, bouncing around in between cars, curbs and medians. I must say, it did help to keep me awake and energized, after barely sleeping the night before.

Riding standing up, without a seat, uses a tremendous amount of energy. I'd be burning about 4,200 kcal/day. As the outside temperature ran up close to 80 degrees F, I began to shed layers to avoid exhaustion and overheating. For both endurance and Asthma Management, I needed to stay well hydrated. I was drinking about 16 ounces of water per hour mixed with an artificial sweetener-free, powdered sports drink to help maintain my electrolyte level. I fueled my body with high calorie energy bars. One every 90 minutes or so. I made it almost 30 miles that first day, with zero Asthma issues and minimal fatigue. At the close of each day, I relied on traditional Irish fare for my recovery protein and much needed calories.

At the end of Day 1, I landed myself in Killadysert, a small village directly west of Limerick (Luimneach in Irish) across the River Shannon. A homey Bed & Breakfast would be my base for the night. I was welcomed by the proprietor, a friendly mid-life Irish woman with a glorious smile and glowing spirit. After finding out what I was doing in Ireland, and why I was touring without a seat, she pumped me full of equal amounts of food, drink and questions. She quickly prepared a huge baked salmon dinner with sweet, white potatoes and fresh vegetables. It was absolutely amazing, even without factoring in my extreme hunger and the fact that all I had in my stomach since leaving the United States were chalky energy bars.

Just when I thought it couldn't get any better...it did. Out came a big, beautiful pint of Guinness. I hadn't asked for it, but as I would soon learn, in Ireland, a request for a pint is assumed, as is the response. Most certainly, yes. Now bear in mind, I had always been a big Guinness fan but this was different. This would be my very first pint on Irish soil and when my host discovered this fact, all hell broke loose. She began calling her family and other guests that were staying in the B&B, to invite them down to the bar to join us. Soon, I was surrounded by village locals, all with pint in hand, toasting to my good health and a successful journey. Then the questions began. Why do you ride standing up? How can you ride with Asthma? Can I try your bike? What do you mean you don't know where you're headed? How can your legs be so small?

That one always gets me. When people first meet me, they almost always look down at my legs. Often with disappointment. Relatively speaking, my legs are nothing special in the world of cycling, walking, or in any other world for that matter. In fact, my dad would joke around and call me chicken legs after I had shaved my legs for competition. He wasn't being mean. He was right. They were and still are, quite chickeny.

In the midst of the mayhem, I thought for a split second about going upstairs to review my maps and pick the following day's route. It soon became clear that my route would not be determined by me, a stranger in a quirky magical land, but by the very locals welcoming me to their kingdom. So I stayed, and drank and drank some more. They were all throwing out ideas for my next day's ride, without me even asking. Nothing I heard quite clicked with me though. It had to feel right, intuitively. Before I knew it, I received all the guidance I could require from one old-timer with coffee/whiskey in hand. Through a thick Irish brogue, he raised his cup with confidence and chopped out, "Molls Gap. Have you gone through there yet? Out to Listowel." I was lucky enough to understand at least this much, through his hearty accent. This was my daily road sign. This much came through loud and clear to me and I was listening. I couldn't wait to leave. They got me so pumped up with Irish stories of hooligans, traditional Irish music and their love of drink, that I was ready to go exploring. I think I would have left at that very moment, if I could have found my bike. I lost track of it some-where between the salmon and Guinness number 4. Several pints later, with many great memories and a full belly of food under my belt, I finally headed upstairs to get some shut-eye, so I'd be ready for the next day's ride. I have no idea what time that was but this would become yet another common theme throughout my time in Ireland. Fuzzy evenings and lost hours.

Ouch. Nothing like waking up in another country with a hangover, knowing you're about to ride a bike without a seat the equivalent of a marathon, maybe more. You know the feeling, right? Well, maybe not. I slowly poured myself down to breakfast where my host from the night before was al-ready up and cooking, with a high-volume spring in both her step and voice. Again, ouch. As I was waiting for my tradi-tional Irish breakfast to be prepared, I questioned my plans to wing it across the Irish countryside. Here I am, with Asthma, riding alone in a foreign country with a headache that could drop a moose. I've got no idea what the roads are like, exactly how far I'll travel or where I'll sleep tonight. Some people would find this unnerving and I must admit, with thoughts of breathing issues from the smoking peat fuel common in this part of the world, a small part of me was con-cerned. A much bigger part of me, however, truly loved and embraced the adventure of it all. Even with fear simmering in the background, the unknown remained my all-embracing traveling buddy, and I welcomed it. Considering the couch I had been unwillingly surfing several years earlier, I wouldn't have had it any other way.

After rushing to finish breakfast and gear up to leave, I went looking for my host. I wanted to check out and say goodbye. I wanted to roll. I needed to roll but, best laid plans, as they say. My search led me out front of the B&B where I not only found my host but also what appeared to be all of her friends and family from all across Ireland. It was unreal. I was mobbed with cheering locals, all with their heavy accents and happy disposition. Their positive energy cured whatever hangover remained and helped feed my confidence for yet another successful stand-up riding day. Wow, I thought. I actually had fans. Well I guess you could call them that. Thousands of miles away from home, no less. It stirred me and would later seed all that was to come, including Team Standing Cyclist. Many months after returning home, I would discover that friends of friends traveling through southwest Ireland would hear tales of an odd American cyclist pub hopping his way from County to County on a bizarre seatless bicycle. I quietly considered what could be done with this sort of attention. I mean, after all, I had never heard of anyone doing anything quite like this. Sure there are Trials riders who tackle obstacles standing up and BMX racers who rarely sit, but this was different. Long distance, adventure cycle touring without a seat is unheard of, I thought. Even though I sincerely enjoyed this style of riding and appreciated how it helped me manage my Asthma challenges, objectively it was still extremely difficult and that attracted attention. What I would do with that attention remained to be seen.

One day after another, much of the same occurred. Town after town, my twisted pseudo celebrity status grew as my legs grew heavy, my lungs screamed and my liver worked double time on the stout. My food rituals soon fell into place. In the absence of energy bars (I ran out about halfway through my trip) I would stuff Irish soda bread in my pack and nibble a bit every hour or so. As they say, when in Rome...eat everything in sight. I desperately needed calories and I must say, the soda bread by day complemented by Guinness each night, although not exactly the diet of an elite athlete, really did the trick. I wasn't relating to either word, elite or athlete, at the time and I still don't. So no mental conflict there. Eat up, drink up, and ride became my Ireland trip mantra.

Up until this point in my standing, rolling meditative practice, big rides or Rolls as I would later call them consisted of several hours of seatless riding totaling no more than 20 to 35 miles per day. Basically one "rolling" marathon give or take 10 miles or so. That was about to change. At the end of day two, I had landed in Listowel. After finding myself a quaint little B&B, I headed out on foot to explore what this crowded touristy town had to offer. Little did I know, my next tour guide would be one of my most important. Caught up in a wave of people shifting into the local tourist office, or Welcome Center as we tend to call them in the U.S.A., I immediately connected with a bold young Irish woman. She was full of piss and vinegar and enough local information to fill a hard drive. I couldn't help recognize the similarities in personality between her and my spunky Irish friend who guided me to this land in the first place. I knew I needed to listen to what she had to say. At first she refused to believe my story. I believe "shite" was her phrase of choice accompanied by other more potent American slangs I shall not repeat here. Eventually, I was able to convince her that I was for real and the ideas began to flow. She would make suggestions in rapid fire succession then stop herself and say, "No, never mind," then move on to the next. Finally, she stopped and said, "You're going to Dingle." Not, I think you might like this village called Dingle or you should check out Dingle. No. In her mind, I was going to Dingle and that was that. The more I asked about this strangely named town, the more she would repeat "Dingle." Well, Dingle it is then. Now mind you, I hadn't seen this town on my map yet so in my mind I questioned whether or not she was putting me on. We said our goodbyes and I was off to dinner, my evening Guinness, and my crinkled maps.

Yes, there was in fact a Dingle. Dingle is a small coastal town on a sizeable peninsula just north of the famous Ring of Kerry tourist route, west of Killarney. My tour guide was on the money. She did leave out one important landmark along the way. Connor Pass. She may have overlooked it, but something tells me, she knew exactly what she was doing.

The following day, the route from Listowel to Dingle led me through a small city called Tralee. It sat roughly at the half-way point between Listowel and Dingle. I stopped in Tralee for a short break and found myself connecting with locals. We discussed my trip, my Asthma, and of course my unusual bicycle. When it was time to move on, I realized I had already clocked about 30 miles that day. I could stay the night in Tra-lee. I could find a cozy B&B, a comfy pub and get an early start the next morning down into Dingle, which was still about 20 miles away. On occasion, all touring cyclists find themselves at these crossroads. If you stay put, you wind up with two short, usually calm, enjoyable days but without much of a mental and physical accomplishment to your credit. If you go on, the challenge you face may push you beyond your limits, to where you just might discover something new about your surroundings and more importantly, your-self. I had to decide and I had to be quick. I thought about my wild woman tour guide back in Listowel. I could hear her voice in my head saying, "What? You want to stop? Shite. No stopping. Dingle! Dingle! Dingle!"

I'd like to say I proceeded with confidence. Brave, comfort-able and prepared. No. Not even close. As I had feared, my Asthma had been acting up from the burning peat used to heat village cottages each evening and my legs were begin-ning to rebel. I had been standing up riding for more than half the day, for the last several days. I was crossing into unex-plored territory. Would this be a win, or turn into the biggest mistake of my life? There was only one way to find out. I bought some extra supplies, stuffed them into my pack, and continued on to Dingle, hoping for the best.

The scenery in this region was especially stunning. Everything was so bright and green. I was surprised to learn, from a local along the way, that my particular year had been drier than usual resulting in far more grays than flowery shades. From what my wide eyes took in, I would have never guessed. This was truly a magical place. You could see it, even feel it.

As the hours passed, I registered a noticeable drop in temperature and big winds began kicking up. Soon I was cycling on narrow, dirt roads surrounded by swift moving two-way traffic. Cars and delivery vans sped around tight curves, and me. The sun dropped low in the sky and then came the gale force horizontal rain. This was getting interesting. It seemed like everyone was in a mad rush to get down to Dingle before nightfall. What did they know that I didn't know? I soon had my answer. Fog. The current tally stood at, rain, high winds, near freezing temperatures (without the wind chill factored in), anxious tourists in sizeable rental cars, narrow cliffside dirt roads, steep ascents, a shortage of food and water and the fact that I was hitting mile 42 standing up.

My legs were screaming. I had rigged my single-speed with two possible rear gears before I left home. In a bind, I could manually place the chain on the larger rear cog to buy me some mechanical advantage in the event of an extra steep hill. It was time to play that card. The chain adjustment required the use of my multi-tool. Partially frozen, numb fingertips made this a tricky task but my efforts paid off. This new gear helped propel me the remaining way to the top of Connor Pass. It was a brutal, yet satisfying, ascent on many levels but the seasoned adventure cyclist in me knew the ride was far from over. Much like a mountaineer successfully ascending a high peak, you're never done until you're back down to base camp.

This day ran much later than I expected. I was running out of daylight and still needed to descend about 5 miles into town. At this point, the fog was so thick that I could hardly see one bike length in front of me. I stopped for a moment to consider a hilltop bivy. In some ways it would be safer but in other ways quite risky. If I descended in the dark without proper front and rear lighting, under this combination of conditions, I risked soaring off the road or getting squashed against the rocks by a tourist looking down to read their map or change their radio station. If I stayed at the top and camped for the night with my limited cold weather gear, I risked hypothermia. The deciding factor for me was food and water. I needed both to help recover from today and to prep me for tomorrow's ride. The decision was made. I would descend.

My first priority was warmth. I needed to maintain my core body temperature. This was not a problem pumping up the pass but riding downhill with limited pedaling, the cold wind would work against me in a big way. Especially standing up. My upright position would catch and direct cold air into my face and chest. Before setting off, I added layers on top and tights down below. I slid both hands into my one spare pair of socks, which would help shield my hands from the cold. If I lost feeling in my hands, braking would become a sketchy proposition or I could slip off my handlebars and fall into traffic. Five miles doesn't seem like much but under these conditions I knew 5 would feel like 20. I was about to drop about 2,000 feet in elevation, down to the sea. I started off riding cautiously with the traffic, with my headlamp attached to my handlebars facing forward. Soon, when my eyes had adjusted to the charcoal mist, I relocated the light to my daypack, facing backward, and set it to flashing mode. My makeshift taillight proved to be a lifesaver. Without it, I am certain I would have been struck from behind or nudged off a cliff.

At times like these, your mind turns from a pile of scattered daydreams and worries to a finely focused laser. It reminded me of downhill mountain biking and the extreme concentration required to stay true and upright through fast and changing terrain. Back then I would always say, "You're not thinking about relationships or paying bills when bombing down ski hill single-track." Every one of my senses were being assaulted. At first, a part of me was terrified but many more parts had never felt so awake, alive and free. After a while it became an exercise in mindfulness and all was well and in flow, inside and out. My bike and I had formed a human-mechanical bond and together we were being piloted by muscle and intuition. Full attention and no attention, all in one. Never had I experienced something quite so natural, so primal. So symphonic.

I ignored the burning in my legs from standing up all day. I forgot about my Asthma, my family and my friends. This was not runner's high, this was do or die. There was no room for error. I continued on like this for over 45 minutes. I couldn't stop and rest. There was no place to stop safely. Until dropping down into town, the roadside shoulder would remain elusive and the other side of the road was a tall rock outcropping that quite often bent into the road. I nearly clipped my shoulder several times.

As town came into view, I thought for a moment about my breathing and how I had come to be riding in this beautiful, frightening, challenging place. What if I had never suffered with Allergic Asthma? Would I be standing up on a single-speed bicycle somewhere in Ireland, alone in the dark, pushing my limits, looking deeply at my life and who I think I am. There was something powerful and fulfilling about my circumstances and every event leading up to them.

I soon rolled into town and through winding alleys, searching for a suitable place to eat and crash for the night. I had just completed the single most difficult cycling session of my life. I was thrilled, but cold, dehydrated and starving. The last thing I was seeking was conversation and "the drink" but this was Ireland after all. Next thing I knew, I was standing in a pub, (still) cold and wet but with a big, fat Guinness in hand. Wherever I went, I continued to be surrounded by friendly, curious locals wanting to buy me a drink and hear my seatless cycling stories. Allergic Asthma would almost always eventually take center stage and I began to use the opportunity to share my issues and how I was overcoming them with others suffering with similar challenges. With parents, kids, anyone interested.

I had a fondness for Ireland and its magical people going into this adventure but on that very night, I fell in love. Until that point, I was a watcher. I was observing what the Irish call Craic, or fun, from the outside looking in at them. That night, I became one of them and experienced real Craic from within their tradition and I would never be quite the same. Before coming here, I would tend to get lost in my own stuff. Ireland helped lead me towards the truth of bigger things and I will be forever grateful.

The next several days had me drifting through cozy villages, small towns and a few congested cities. I continued my Adventure Way approach of letting my acquaintances and my surroundings guide the next leg of my journey. It never failed me. Each day was more exciting and meaningful then the last. I rode along Dingle Bay in the crisp morning air, through Castlemaine, Kilorglin and toured ancient castle grounds in Killarney. I made friends in virtually every area I passed through. Near Inch, I met a young Israeli man and his girlfriend. They were bright and adventurous and were obsessed with my standing cycle. They were the only people in Ireland I let ride my bike, even for a minute. It was tough for them at first to adjust but they soon got the hang of it and were sad to give it back. I wandered through a very old cemetery near Killarney. It was a chilling experience. There were not only headstones of interest but also ancient ruins scattered throughout the property. I felt oddly at home. In fact, during my entire time in Ireland I had that same warm, homey, protected feeling. Like I was being welcomed back to my childhood home by loving parents, even when things got a little creepy.

One night while heading out of my rural B&B, for a good meal in town, the front door opened on its own right in front of me. Now mind you, this was an ancient, thick wooden eight-foot door that had to have weighed hundreds of pounds. There was no automation, wind and no people nearby. When she heard the squeal of old hinges, the owner called out from across the kitchen about thirty feet away. I hollered back, telling her what had happened. She wasn't surprised at all. Even then, with chills and all, I felt quite at home as I wandered off into the darkness.

Perhaps my final day in Ireland was my finest. That day, I would meet my own personal historian, tour guide and teacher. Sean had a tremendous impact on my life at that time, and to this day. I had just arrived in Limerick and was passing by a local pub. Sean was sitting alone at a sidewalk table. He stood up and greeted me as if he had been expecting me. That was the beginning of a very long night of stories, lessons, advice, Guinness and many new friends. Sean couldn't know I was still grieving the loss of my father. He couldn't know my relatively new marriage had recently imploded or about my struggles with breathing. He knew nothing about the conflicting emotions that stirred in my brain. Emotions involving loved ones suffering through significant loss and how I wished to ease their pain, but felt I was failing miserably. But somehow he knew. He seemed to know it all, before I even arrived. Before long, we were opening up to one another and it was liberating beyond description.

At one point, I began to talk about what I had accomplished over the past week. I would proudly describe my journey, riding standing up, meeting people and drinking my way around the countryside. From deep within his calming, warm demeanor he would abruptly, at times aggressively, interrupt me and redirect the conversation toward something more meaningful. He had no interest in my cycling, my breathing issues or who I thought I was. He was the first and only person in Ireland I could say that about. Every time my ego reared its head, even a little, and I began to describe the intensity of my adventure, he would cut in and change the subject. He knew there was much more to this trip than muscle and miles, image and bragging rights. He told me that my open mind and willingness to let go and allow this country to guide me where I needed to go, had been of great importance and to remain focused on those points of experience.

He took me to a pub that he, his "fodder" and "granfodder" had all frequented over a span of 100 years. It was a fantastic experience. He introduced me to many people, always referring to me as his friend, never mentioning what I was doing in Ireland or how he had just met me only hours before. Sean opened up about the loss of his beloved and I opened up about my dad. I explained how I felt responsible for my mom now that my dad is gone, but that I didn't feel ready for that responsibility. I exposed my anguish and guilt over several, deeply loving but failed relationships that required more of me than I was able to give. I told this relative stranger that in some ways I was hanging by a very thin thread. I told him things I hadn't told my closest friends and family members in fear it would weaken their image of me. I gave him details and I was completely comfortable doing so. Completely vulnerable. He listened intently with a knowing I cannot properly describe here, then grabbed my arm firmly, leaned in, and said simply in his beautiful brogue, "It is our burden to bear."

He broke down giving and receiving, suffering and pleasure, coping and clarity, ending every sentence with a charming "Says I." I was being guided in ways I had never expected. He went on, implying we all share a challenging path that cannot be avoided. That it's just who we are, all of us, and we must be true to that or we are not real at all. That, if we deny our suffering, we deny our truth, left with living a life of illusion. A life of real misery, today and always. We must engage our adversity with full heart and mind. That is our ultimate truth and purpose. I felt a chill run *up* my spine and everything changed. It was an electric shock of reality and an important second-half-of-life foreshadowing. A deep, universal teaching. A shift we are all capable of and perhaps designed for. I felt acceptance, equanimity, and I settled peacefully into myself. Maybe it was the thick stout. Maybe it was something more. I learned so much about life from Sean in such a short time. Life's teachings and teachers come in all forms, but I continue to find they always come when needed the very most.

My Ireland is now a fond memory. I arrived filled with doubt, some fear and a patch of despair hidden deep inside. I left a different person. I left a Standing Cyclist. More importantly, I left my helplessness and, at the same time, a tiny chunk of ego behind. It was time to face and appreciate the privilege of my challenges, burdens and responsibilities with confidence and comfort, and I was ready.

After returning home from Ireland, I had much to sort out. Relationships, money issues and a growing pile of so called adult responsibilities foreign to me in younger years. I had set out seeking adventure and returned to face more of the same, but much heavier than peddling a bike. Real life adventures involving family, career, ongoing Asthma Management challenges and the return of my underlying lower back problems. My back pain soon became my nemesis. There were times I couldn't carry my laptop bag to a business meeting. I couldn't even pick it up off the ground to swing the strap over my shoulder. Driving was especially tortuous. I couldn't sit, stand or sleep for very long without having to shift positions. My back pain took several forms. One resembled Sciatica which is typically caused by the pinching of a nerve resulting in a shooting, stabbing pain which runs from the lower back down the backside of one leg. For me that was my left leg. The other form was a sharp pain at the base of my back that acted up when bending to pick anything up off the ground. I was always used to doing for myself, never needing assistance. As the weeks went by, I had to rely more on others to help dress me and wash up, and to assist with simple house chores. This was a very vulnerable time for me and I experienced many teachings.

I've never been big on doctors and medication but enough was enough. I sought out and visited several different physicians and specialists. They were all saying the same thing. Again, they believed I had a disk issue and that I needed physical therapy and possibly surgery. Being a troubleshooter at heart I couldn't leave it at that. I needed to identify a cause before I could go after a reasonable long-term solution. I traced back my activities to hardcore mountain biking, roller hockey and other body stressing sports I had partaken in for many years. Also, the off-road recumbent tour in Montana certainly stressed my back and helped set the stage, but was there even more to it than that?

I felt great during my training for the Ireland tour but immediately after is when the worst of the pain kicked in. How could this be? I followed my symptoms backward in time to my riding style throughout the hilly Irish countryside. I had ridden standing on a single-speed bike. I revisited my riding position, trip journal and several videos I had taken during training prior to the trip. Then it all clicked. To overcome the short, steep hills without a wide range of gears, I had to frequently yank up on the handlebars while pressing down on the pedals. Now any cyclist will know this is not terribly unusual but due to my unique standing position, this was occurring with my back more upright than normal. I was hyperextending my back and I was doing it with great force, repeatedly throughout the trip. The medical professionals agreed.

Around this time, I had officially established my Standing Cyclist website and was sharing my trip data and Asthma Management techniques via the internet and by networking with Asthma sufferers around the globe. The spark I experienced in Ireland was now a small, growing flame. My focus was shifting from my own challenges to helping others cope with and manage their own. My life was changing for the better but in some ways it was worse than before. The months were passing by quickly and not only was I unable to ride, I was barely able to walk. My physical activity was limited to stretching. I noticed my lack of exercise was working against my Asthma Management. My fitness level was falling off and my symptoms were returning with greater frequency. I felt like I was going backward. My body was failing and I was afraid, before long, I would lose the mental strength and confidence I had gained in Ireland. The idea of that Standing Cyclist going out again on a trip was a distant pipe dream. I was losing momentum and once again thought about giving up. I had lost a year to severe back pain and was losing hope. How would I get going again and how long would it take? Would I get going again?

This long, slow period of experimentation and recovery had become a huge obstacle to overcome and it seemed to be taking forever. I was terribly impatient. It was driving me nuts. In hindsight, this period slowed me down in every way and, as it turned out, that was a good thing. I was juggling too many things. They all twisted together and impacted one another. A huge To-Do list, lack of sleep and money, and a growing shortness of breath really plays with your head. If you're not dug in deep, you're not dug in at all. It forced me to go deep, seek balance, and be better.

Slowly, very slowly, I expanded my stretching routines to include light walks. I found a beautiful, short trail along a dam at one of the largest man-made lakes in Pennsylvania, not far from my home. I would work at my computer by day, while standing up to ease my back pain, then drive to the trail and walk until sunset. Week after week, I increased my pace.

Soon the winter moved in and the cold air became a breathing consideration which oddly enough, and thankfully, distracted me a little from the pain shooting down my butt and leg. By mid-winter I was post-holing in deep snow across that dam, without any serious back or breathing issues. It was during these cold, windy training sessions that I began to daydream about my next Standing Cyclist adventure. I felt my recovery was testing my patience. That was nothing compared to what was to come.

Chapter 6 - ICELAND

I was always interested in polar regions and thought how challenging it would be to go on a seatless cycling expedition in a chilling, remote location such as Antarctica or up north in the Yukon. After researching the possibilities for several months, Greenland became the obvious choice. An old military base and permafrost trails would provide the perfect combination of isolation, endurance, adventure and spiritual exploration. I put a plan together and stepped up my training. The universe had other plans for me, though. When it came time for me to purchase my airline tickets, I was informed that due to a lack of interest, flights from the U.S. to northwest Greenland (my target area) were no longer available. I would have to fly to Greenland via Europe at four times the cost. At this point in my life, this was not an option. I went back to the drawing board and revisited my second choice, Iceland. It was a fast decision and one I would not regret.

I've always felt that my choice of bicycle touring destinations held great meaning. That trip was no exception. Iceland would prove to be a brutal test of my ability to travel alone, in severe weather, in my now typical seatless, standing cycling position. Everything was difficult. Even simple things like cooking (in cold, wet 50 mph winds) resulted in great frustration. My patience was stretched thinner than ever and working through that became the official theme of this particular trip. For me, this adventure was the ultimate practice in patience. This trip isolated me, slowed me down, and gave me no choice but to look deep inside, remain calm, and be very patient with myself and my surroundings. Surroundings and outside influences, outside of my control. I had much to learn about patience, tolerance and letting go, and how all three interrelate.

In terms of difficulty and lessons learned, one day stands out the most. I had to cover 40 miles seatless over a mountain pass in strong winds, with gear. For hours, gusts would toss me off my bike and into a ditch along the roadside. Each time I had to retune my brain, reorganize my panniers, remount and get rolling once again into the high winds and driving horizontal rain. Talk about patience. After a while I was humbled by Mother Nature's attempt to demolish me. At least that's what it felt like. Eventually, I was broken like a young, restless horse would be broken by an expert ranch hand. I settled into that new role with an odd sort of relief. I let go. It felt a bit like a breath of fresh air when you needed it the most. Later that night, I thought about the gift I had been given and felt thankful for the opportunity to bend and grow. More about this later on.

I approached my Iceland prep much as I had before, for previous bikepacking trips. I always try to recognize teachings from prior experiences, both good and bad, on and off the bike. One very big lesson I learned from Montana, Ireland and my resulting body damage, was to tour with a multispeed drivetrain. The simplicity of a single-speed had its advantages but in my upright riding position, I needed the added mechanical advantage of a full range of gears when touring up and down killer hills, with loaded panniers. I knew I'd be spending much of my time on-road but significant time off-road as well. I needed to configure my Iceland rig to handle just about anything. For this trip, I built up a fairly standard mountain bike with front and rear racks, 24-speeds, 26" wheels, and off-road tires. I built in my normal Standing Cyclist features such as a raised cockpit, strong BMX handlebars, open downhill mountain bike pedals, and of course no seatpost or seat. I tested out several frame geometries and settled on a medium size with a fairly relaxed, laid back, head tube angle.

In early 2008, I had finished the Iceland bike and was in full training mode. I was standing for 10 to 20 miles per riding session and rode about 5 days/week. My riding position was spot-on and the bike was holding up well in the woods and along my curvy Pennsylvania roads. My Sciatica and lower back pain were almost completely gone and my Asthma appeared to be under control although, with Asthma, you can never really tell how under control your breathing truly is. That's the part that plays with your mind. It's a must to sort out those thoughts in training. There's no place for negativity and fear once you're out bike tripping, solo, in lava fields and high winds. I needed to push myself hard while local under controlled circumstances to best prepare myself and to know just how my muscles and emotions will react when it matters most. When I'm over there alone in the gnarly Icelandic countryside.

One month before my departure to Iceland, I began organizing and testing my gear. Ireland was cushy compared to what awaited me in Iceland. B&B's and fine stout would be replaced by cold, hard ground, an ultralight emergency sleeping sack, my small bivy tent and freeze dried camp food. Once again, I intended to wear one set of clothes and pack one additional set, plus two jackets. One middle layer for warmth and one outer layer to cut the wind and rain. I'd be wearing supportive yet pliable hiking boots, waterproof and slightly oversized to accommodate my thick mountaineering socks. I would be traveling light, relative to traditional bike touring standards, but my gear still tipped the scales at 45 lbs. with food, water and camp fuel included. Ah, the cooking dilemma. I knew I'd be riding through remote areas where gas cartridges for my compact, well-used camp stove would be hard to come by. I opted for a high altitude liquid fuel stove, which added weight but was better suited to various weather conditions and could burn different types of local fuel, even everyday gasoline.

My book of choice for this trip would be *Walking the Gobi* by Helen Thayer. This amazing story chronicles Helen and her husband's journey, on foot, across one of the largest, hottest deserts on the planet. Ironically, this book would prove to be an essential piece of gear, during my chilling time in Iceland. Truly inspiring.

Even though I had scheduled the trip for Iceland's summer season, I knew that the weather in the more mountainous, volcanic regions would be cold, windy and possibly quite wet and foggy. I looked back on my unnerving Connor Pass experience in Ireland, two years earlier. What would I be getting myself into this time, I thought. I continued to work through my fears, planned for the worst, and hoped for the best.

I scheduled a flight from JFK airport in New York to Keflavik airport in southwest Iceland. Keflavik sits adjacent to a former NATO airbase and is just under 35 miles away from Iceland's capital city of Reykjavik. Once again, my game plan was no game plan. My buddy Brian would be driving me, my boxed bicycle and camping gear, to the airport. Six hours later, after crossing the Atlantic crammed in coach between tourists and business travelers, I would land in Keflavik after midnight. From there, it was all about The Adventure Way. You've got to have a calm, open mind to roll like this. Once uncertainty morphs into fear, the signs are missed and your brain deceives you. You end up making bad decisions that could lead to disappointment or even injury. You become your own worst enemy. You must make friends, even become lovers, with the unknown. Of course you must remain cautious but never paranoid. Basically, learn when and how to get out of your own way and the rest will work itself out quite well. In flow. A good way to approach life, for me anyway.

Okay, so it's Friday, August 22, 2008 about 1am local time. Here I am standing in an airport in Iceland surrounded by gear bags and a big box filled with pieces of what would soon carry me past vast volcanic fields and geothermal springs, and all I can think about is food and beer. I'm starved but I can't leave my stuff. I manage to drag my gear around to exchange my money for the local, Icelandic currency and run some other airport errands. Eventually, I board a shuttle headed for the main bus terminal in Reykjavik. Perfect. This will work just fine. What I mean by that, I have no idea. I still have no plan, no map of the city, no sleep under my belt and no place to build my bike and stage my gear. A lot of "no's" but no problem. This was part of the fun and the challenge of it all.

Once settled in, I decided to get a little shut-eye on the bus to the city. I was feeling at peace, did a brief meditation and said a simple prayer to set things off right. I was mentally well balanced, spiritually grounded, and ready for anything. Unless of course anything meant a pack of well-off, drunken, rowdy American twentysomethings heading to Reykjavik for their buddy's bachelor party. Apparently Rekyavik has quite a global reputation as a party town. Who knew? So I'm sitting there quietly listening to their rants and cheers, laced with nasty English profanities concerning shots of booze and Icelandic strippers, as an innocent little Icelandic girl and her mother sitting across from me begin to cringe. My mind went from calm to disturbed to good old fashioned pissed off. I could, I should, do something about this. After all, this wouldn't be the first time I held my own with a bunch of but-theads, bigger than me. Of course, this would be the first time I would do it sober. Just when I was about to stand up and probably get my ass kicked, the little girl looked at her mom and me and said in broken English with a long sigh, "Huhhhfff...Americans, all so mean," shaking her head in sad-ness and disappointment. Instead of throwing gasoline on the fire, I sat back, diffused my anger and sent a simple grin her way and mumbled, "We're not all like that." She blushed and smiled back, and all was once again right with the world. The boys had settled down and I remained in one piece, no blood, no concussion. Ironically, 10 years earlier, I could have easily been one of those clueless, disrespectful Neander-thals.

The bus dumped us all out at the main city bus terminal around 2am. I needed to build my bike, gear up and figure out where to store my bike box for the return trip home. There were lockers at the terminal but they could not be ac-cessed until the terminal office opened at 4am. I took the time in between to piece together my seatless wonder then nap amongst the homeless and scattered locals scheduled to catch the first bus of the day out of town. I also needed to buy liquid fuel to fill the canister that would run my stove for the coming week. Someone tipped me off to a city campground that provided backpackers with fuel and also disposed of used canisters (good info for the return trip home). This valuable intel would automatically lead me through the city via my best possible route and, by chance, seeded the next leg of my trip.

With the sun still resting below the horizon, I was finally ready to roll. My steed was built, panniers loaded, water bottles and energy bars cued up for action and my bike box sat safely in a rental locker until I returned the following week. Off I went, attempting to navigate the city streets using a map written in the quite confusing local language. The glow from my headlamp lit the way through the shadows between street lights. Coasting a little, pedaling a little, always standing, I picked up speed and soaked in the buzz of soaring through narrow alleys and intersections in this foreign land in the semi-lit haze on two hours of sleep. I was only riding for ten minutes before the sight of my stand-up touring bike caught the attention of the local police. I think at first they believed I had stolen the bike, since there was no seat and I was moving with a purpose. After I explained what I was doing in Iceland and how I would be riding without a seat the entire time, I received a blank stare from both of them. It seemed they thought I was delusional or maybe my story was simply lost in translation. Icelandic is a complex language with few if any similarities to English.

On this trip I was riding with two new pieces of gear. I was still riding with my heart rate monitor to help me keep my

Asthma in check but now on the same wrist I was also wearing a Road ID bracelet. This, now popular means to identify you and any major health issues you may have, was fairly new at the time. All of your records can be accessed by emergency personnel on the web and telephone, using the code at the back of the bracelet, in the event you are injured and cannot speak. It's a wonderful invention that I wear on every trip and training ride. The second addition was a SPOT satellite transmitter. This little high tech wonder has become my riding partner in both the U.S. and abroad. It tracks your position via satellite and transmits and posts your position periodically on the web. You can also manually send a distress signal from most locations in the world, which will notify local search and rescue personnel in case of a life threatening emergency. It's great for peace of mind when undertaking a solo, endurance challenge while managing health issues such as Asthma. Later, during my Standing Cyclist fundraising and tribute rides, SPOT trip data would help supporters track my progress and arrange for newspaper and television interviews, to help raise awareness for special causes. It's a wonderful gadget I have come to appreciate a great deal.

You might say that packing bike tools, using a Road ID bracelet, a SPOT tracker and following maps is in conflict with The Adventure Way. I beg to differ. My TAW "way" is about free-rolling as I tend to call it. You go as you go. Then, all is as it is. You do some common sense planning upfront as preparation to ensure you get started successfully, and you consider safety measures and supplies. You may use a map to avoid a dangerous route but you do not overthink, overplan or overreact. You never disturb the natural flow or dilute the essence of the experience. TAW is not about taking unnecessary risks, thrill seeking or bragging rights. It's simply about old fashion adventure and the lessons and warm relationships that result. Some hobos walk, some roll. Some are low tech, some high tech. It all works.

On this particular adventure, I was seriously limited on time. I had exactly one week, including travel time, which was tight for any international bicycle excursion, let alone an unpredictable and unplanned Standing Cyclist trip. I had to be back in Keflavik for my return flight to JFK on August 28th. I had important personal and professional commitments the day after my return flight, so falling short of this departure was not an option. Having time constraints when traveling in this loose mode can be unnerving. I would do my best to cope with the challenge.

After filling up my camp stove fuel canisters, my next pit stop was for chow. A hot chocolate and Panini from a local cafe were the perfect combination to satisfy both my brain and belly. As usual and intended, I had not yet decided my next move. The large volcano, Snaefellsjokull, sitting at the tip of the Snaefellsnes Peninsula had caught my interest after discovering its rich storyline and chatting with English speaking locals upon my arrival. This ominous looking mountain was made famous in both books and movies. It was considered adjacent to the Westfjords, an area of passing interest for me before leaving home, located several days north of my current location. Things began to subtlety drift into place. Overall, this route made sense but still no solid plan materialized.

On my first full day, after catching an Adventure Way vibe from some European backpackers at the city campground, I decided to make my way from Reykjavik to Akranes. As I would soon discover, this would not be easy. There was a "no bikes" tunnel, 10 miles long through Hvalfjordur Bay, connecting the two cities. There was an overland route to the east, but I was afraid I'd use up too much trip time since I was low on sleep and still unfamiliar with my surroundings. If I attempted this route and fell short, it could jeopardize my entire trip. I opted for the tunnel and began to ride in that general direction. While riding, I reflected on the knowns and unknowns and on the danger. I've grown to trust my intuition in both work and my personal life and my little voice was now screaming loud and clear, don't do it! I discovered a bus route that ran between the two cities, carrying commuters and even bicycles safely through the tunnel. I bought a ticket and was soon on my way through, deep beneath the bay. It became clear, very soon, that I had made the right choice. The tunnel was extremely narrow and curvy with two lanes of high speed traffic running in opposite directions. There was absolutely no shoulder to ride on. There was limited lighting and the shadows cast between fast moving headlights gave it a dizzying disco feel. The 10-minutes through the tunnel felt like forever and proved more highly charged than crossing the Atlantic one day after the crash of a Spanish airliner, news of which I had heard while waiting to depart from JFK to Iceland. I would later discover that this tunnel had a deadly track record. Numerous backpackers and cyclists had been killed over the years and, not long before my trip, one touring cyclist had been killed attempting to navigate the long, dark arterial. My little voice had served me well.

After arriving in Akranes, I proceeded to get lost. I should be used to that by now. When you wander around a foreign country, without a rigid plan, losing your way is kind of a given. I've since learned to embrace and enjoy it rather than fight it, fear it, or get frustrated and impatient with my circumstances and surroundings. That gets you nowhere, except more lost. Besides, there's a lot to be learned from deep within the unknown. That's where some of life's best stories and teachings hide.

Eventually a local tipped me off about a primitive campsite across town. Turns out, it sat by the water's edge and was fairly open to the elements. Soon the wind and rain would kick up and almost rip the rainfly off my compact, one man bivy tent, but not before I was to taste a little local singletrack. I may be a standing road cyclist but my craving for tight, fast, and dirty switchbacks is always there. I couldn't resist it. Still fully loaded with gear, I hit another 8 miles of riding, along the water, following that beautiful little trail between grapefruit sized rocks and grassy rolling hills. I was sleepy but the energy feed of where I was, and what I was doing at that very moment, moved my arms and legs seemingly without my own conscious intervention. I was having a moment, the first of many memorable Iceland moments.

Laying in my tent alone, getting hammered by high winds, dropping temps and horizontal rain, I began to think about what most Asthma sufferers think about when they are riding their bikes alone all day, standing up, in a foreign land. "I really hope I don't bite it." I mean, you have to consider the possibility. Before I left home, I had thought about this extensively. I even updated my Last Will and Testament and left a little "just in case" note for family and friends, hoping of course it wouldn't be needed...on this trip anyway. Along with my fears and doubts, the underlying trip theme of patience began to unfold as well.

For the most part, Iceland is a cold, wet, windy and very isolated place. Its ominous beauty is matched by its ever-present uncertainty. It seems like everything is more difficult here, unforgiving, and requires robust forbearance to work through it effectively. The Icelandic people come from a long line of strong, resilient, self-sufficient loners. Unlike my adventures through our own western states and Ireland where everyone you meet is open, curious and helpful, here you don't feel "seen". Most of the questions and friendly conversations I experienced in Iceland were with foreigners. That's not to say Icelanders are not helpful and friendly. They most certainly are, when you can find them. Once I left the city of Reykjavik, I felt as if I was leaving this Earth. Surrounded by lava fields and the single largest group of active volcanos in the world, you feel as if you're all alone and riding on the moon. You feel like you must depend 100% on yourself for your survival. Of course this isn't the case (entirely), but it sure can feel that way. You must learn to be patient with the people and weather patterns, and most importantly, with yourself.

I spent many hours alone with my own heartbeat, pedal rhythms and thoughts. The evening hours were the most interesting. Sleeping outside alone, away from campers and city folk, in such an isolated area is good fuel for deep insight. You become very aware of your body and your mind. Every ache, pain, fear and failure stops by for a visit. Sometimes all at once. With practice, you eventually gain the ability to simply watch them rather than become their victim. My ongoing meditation practice had helped me with that, and continued to develop, during that cycling retreat. That trip was already proving to be an inner growth experience, within the context of the barren, natural world that surrounded me mile after mile, night after night. Character development, by fire.

Laying there one night, I remembered a private outburst I had back home. I lost my patience with something I can't even recall now, but it caused me to swing my left arm out into the air in anger and frustration. There was no contact, nothing to hit, but something shifted within my shoulder and pain shot down my arm to my wrist and fingers. It was excruciating. This was two weeks before my flight to Iceland, and I was panicked. What an idiot, I thought. I may have just jeopardized my entire trip and for what? Why? Because I lost it over some silly circumstance that would surely pass. This pain would remain with me throughout my journey in Iceland. It served as a constant reminder to me to practice patience and mindful action. There were times during that trip when I thought the pain would hold me back or even cause me to bail out, but it didn't ever get quite that bad. It sat beneath the surface just noticeable enough to keep me thinking about what matters the most when challenged in this way. To sit well in the storm, whatever that storm may be. To stop and look deeply at the impatience and intolerance. To see them for what they really are and not act upon them in negative ways. To this day, this remains an important part of my daily spiritual practice. Looking back, I greatly value those long days in Iceland, riding alone, against the wind and cold rain. The journey started out as a simple challenge and adventure. It ended up being a gift that has continued to bring great joy and peace into my life to this day. Much like Ireland has, but with a slightly different spin.

Two different chapters, of equal importance, within the same book of soul experiences.

On Saturday the 23rd, I decided to head up north to Borgarnes. By the close of that day, I would cover 31 miles without any significant Asthma incidents. My route would track through beautiful coastal scenery, and the weather and riding conditions would continue to push my limits. Later I found, according to my heart rate monitor, that I had burned almost 5,000 kcal and my heart rate averaged 124 beats per minute throughout an 8-hour day while riding in my stand-up position. This combination of statistics would remain fairly consistent throughout my time in Iceland. Other constants would include cold temps, wet clothes, no camp fires (no trees to burn), energy draining headwinds and dangerous crosswinds, and of course that ever present feeling of great isolation.

To help cope with my time away from family and friends, I decided to leave the clock on my heart rate monitor set to home time instead of changing it to local Iceland time, as I normally would. It was comforting, during tough riding sessions, to glance down at my wrist and consider what everyone was doing right then at that moment. Still sleeping? Eating dinner, I'll bet. Maybe warm and cozy, kicked back watching TV. Comforting for a moment but it was soon back to the business at hand. That business being, a high output while trying to not get blown off the road.

The wind in Iceland was my biggest surprise and my greatest challenge. Riding standing up instead of tucked down low increased my drag even under normal circumstances. I trained standing up and knew how this effected my speed and endurance even in high winds, but Pennsylvania wind is not Iceland wind. During that trip, I regularly experienced 40 to 60 mph winds, seemingly coming from all directions, alternating turns. It was like a game or even a conspiracy. Yes, paranoia was setting in. It was clearly a concerted effort amongst the elements to beat the shit out of me. Riding standing up, with loaded panniers, was like riding with sails raised to catch the wind, both headwinds and crosswinds. Later, near the great Snaefellsjokull volcano, these winds would shift from nuisance to dangerous.

At first the ride to Borgarnes was uneventful, however, this smooth flow did not last long. A cold rain pelted me from all sides and slowed my pace considerably. I could usually average around 7 mph, standing, but was now challenged to even break 7 mph momentarily. I could have run faster than that, if I was a runner, which I most certainly am not. I've always rolled much better than I could trot. Now, riding standing up, I feel I've captured both modes of transportation in one rolling motion. This would become more evident several years down the road when I would begin training and tripping on a standing, fixed-gear (no coasting) touring bike. Truly a blend of both disciplines. This remains my favorite, most comfortable cycling style to this day.

As both an experienced meditator and Asthma sufferer, I try to stay mindful of my breath and how my mind and body respond or sometimes react to breathing incidents. You may have noticed by now, I call them incidents. This is because the word attack is not quite accurate in my particular case. I have never (yet) been hospitalized or had a life threatening Asthma attack as so many other adults and far too many children suffer every day, around the world. My heart truly goes out to them. My hope has always been that my journey and methods may benefit others in some small way.

When I accidentally experience a trigger I immediately become hypersensitive to what may happen to me, as many would. In my mind, to help cope with this, I immediately remove myself from the physical experience by simply watching the event and my emotions. Through intense practice, I watch what is happening rather than be consumed by what may happen. I don't allow myself to get caught up in it. This helps dissolve the fear and the worry. Also, I see things as they are in that moment instead of how they could be. This positions me very well to work through the physical aspect of my Asthma which includes the classic airway inflammation and obstruction most all Asthma sufferers experience. I focus on my breath. I watch it, I do not try to control it. With practice, this has helped me to lower my heart rate and ease my symptoms, on demand. My mindfulness meditation practice, along with many other techniques, has helped me to manage my Asthma without daily medication. Many people of course require daily preventative and rescue treatments to stay functional and safe. If you and your doctor feel this is your best course of action, by all means, continue on this path. In addition, however, I would recommend learning and practicing mindfulness meditation as a supplement to traditional Western treatments. This ancient practice, although associated with Buddhism, is not in its purest form restricted to any one religious or wisdom tradition. Today, there are many wonderful resources available in print, audio, video and also by joining a local meditation group. I am constantly expanding my practice which now incorporates other Eastern techniques and includes staff walking (rhythmic power walking and hiking with a tall walking stick) and standing cycling on my fixed-gear bicycle which I consider a marvelous meditation-in-motion. I refer to this style of riding meditation as "Rolling", but more about this later.

My journey to Borgarnes led me to the infamous Ring Road. This well-traveled road, known as Route 1, is Iceland's main thoroughfare connecting together all major towns and cities. Not the best road for cyclotouring as I would soon discover. I wasn't even sure bicycles were allowed along this stretch. I decided to chance it. I would be following this route for about 12 miles. No sweat, right? Wrong. The wind regularly tossed me into traffic and also into the gully alongside the highway. Soon I got tired of picking myself and my loaded bike back up only to be beaten down again, so I decided to ride the cow path which ran alongside the same ditch. This challenging single-track trail appealed to my mountain biking roots. I was loving it, but my fun came with a price. My heart rate was running way higher than it should and together with rich farm odors and tall grass, increased my chances of an Asthma incident. My HR monitor indicated I had burned over 1,000 kcal more than expected. My caloric intake/hydration/heart rate/Allergic Asthma trigger balance point was now, way off. I needed to consider a different route and fast.

By now, the weather had worsened. The crosswinds had increased in intensity and the rain shifted from vertical to horizontal. I could no longer keep my eyeglasses dry enough to see. I considered removing them but my nearsightedness would have made dodging obstacles and surfing the waves of mud along my off-road path, especially while standing up, near impossible. I was losing traction, literally spinning my wheels, and finally pulled off to reassess my route. Keeping my maps, and everything else, shielded from the cold rain was an ongoing challenge. Iceland is a very open landscape. I was used to being surrounded by trees and other makeshift forms of shelter while out adventuring back home in the states. Here, my own jacket and bivy tent were my only reliable options. After checking out the surrounding roads on my soggy map, my heart sank. My best alternate route spurred off about 5 miles behind me. I was hurting on many levels. Backtracking was the last move I wanted to make. Every mile was so damn difficult. How could I consider going backward? All athletes and touring cyclists want to proceed forward. No one ever wants to go backward but, of course, sometimes we have to step back to discover what's ahead. I made the tough call and reversed my focus. Halfway back, I ran into another cyclotourist. A welcomed connection at just the right time. He was familiar with my original Ring Road route and advised I continue with my initial game plan and not go back further to pick up the alternate route. He explained how the alternate route would take me two times longer to ride in these poor weather conditions. Funny how life works. We met while crossing an intersection. One-minute sooner or later and we would not have met at all. My day would have turned out quite differently. Synchronicity strikes again. Once again, I reversed my direction and continued on my way toward Borganes following the challenging Ring Road route.

This reminded me of an occurrence, many years before. I had gone through a period of high stress both at home and at work. I was hypersensitive, very impatient and angry. One evening driving back to Pennsylvania from my work in New Jersey, I experienced a memorable lesson about patience and how things usually happen for a reason. I would later call the story, The Dollar and the Pen and referenced it frequently in my business coaching practice. I was dodging traffic, in the dark and rain, and was approaching a busy toll booth about one-hour north of NYC. I was anxious to get home and couldn't bear the thought of anything that might impair my progress. Just then, I dropped my last dollar bill in the gap between the driver's seat and center console. It was too far down for me to reach without pulling off the road. I flipped out. In one moment, I experienced the full gamete of negative emotions. Surprise, anxiety, panic, frustration, self-pity, anger...the works. Why me? How could this horrible little dollar do this to me? What have I done to deserve this shit? I scrambled to find enough loose change to make it through the toll booth without incident. Got it. Whew. I continued on my way. I still didn't really "get it", though. I still didn't see how absurd and unattractive my behavior was, especially over something so ridiculous. I continued to drive and wonder, why me? My own view of the situation (negative history) and reality (positive potential) simply didn't match up, but I didn't recognize this at the time. I couldn't open my eyes wide enough to see even the possibility of a bigger picture.

When I finally arrived home and pulled into my driveway, I gathered my things and readied myself to exit the car and begin my evening decompression at home. Just then, I must have caught the pen that sat in my shirt pocket with my sleeve. I struggled to grab it as it launched up and spun through the air and, for what seemed like minutes, danced around the cockpit of my Volkswagen until finding its home in the very same crack as the dollar whose loss I had still not completely recovered from. I wanted to cry. This was my favorite pen. I used this pen every day. I had traveled with it all around the world for both business and pleasure. I had thought the inconvenience of the dollar slipping from my grasp was difficult but this would be life changing. Earth shattering. My lucky pen was gone. It was so special. I couldn't move.

I just sat there in a state of shock until the absurdity of it all cracked me up and I couldn't stop giggling. Totally disarmed, I bent down and looked under my seat. What I saw astonished me. There was my pen, nestled snugly inside the open dollar bill. The bill cradled my prized pen as a mama would cradle her babe. That bill was in the right place at the right time. If it didn't land exactly where it did before my pen went flying, the narrow pen would have fallen down behind and beneath the bracket that held the driver's seat in place, gone forever. What originally appeared to be misfortune was actually a gift. If I had been calmer, more patient and open to the situation, I would have avoided much suffering. Iceland was turning out to be The Dollar and the Pen in full blown touring action. Each day, more difficult, wetter and colder than the last but with something profound in tow. Was I being tested? I prefer to think I was being taught. I was in school and was opening more and more each day to the opportunities and teachings placed before me. Far from awake but at least traveling with eyes wide open.

Fifteen miles later, I finally approached the town of Borganes but between me and the main street through town ran a long bridge with no rideable shoulder and plenty of traffic. The wind and rain at this point was accompanied by dense fog. Visibility was ridiculously low and, between standing up and the cold, I could barely feel my legs. They had passed the point of pain and now felt like they belonged to someone else. This was probably a good thing. One less thing to focus on. All my brain would have to do is tell that other fellow to keep moving his legs and we'd be in town before we knew it. Providing no local commuter would clip me with their side view mirror along the way. After carefully crossing the narrow bridge, I spotted a fast food joint and downed a burger and fries like it was my last meal. I kept one eye on my loaded bike which was leaning against the corner of the building, in the pouring rain.

I cruised around Borganes exploring the territory and chatting with whatever locals I could find in the raging storm. I received a few tips on navigating the tricky side streets but nothing yet on a place to squat for the night. I thought about continuing on but between my energy level, the weather and time of day, this would have been a bad move. I wouldn't have made it far before running out of juice or as they say in cycling circles, bonking. I've been there many times but low blood sugar and fatigue plus breathing issues can make for a serious trio of challenges not to be taken lightly.

Thanks to one subtle piece of advice, I found myself passing a primitive camping area alongside a small body of water, just on the edge of town. That would be my home for the night. At last, I thought I could warm up, rest up and settle in for the night but sitting in a raging storm without anything to burn would make starting a campfire highly unlikely. I knew changing into my (not so wet) second set of clothes and heating water with my camp stove, was my next best option for maintaining my core body temperature but I couldn't change and squeeze into my single person bivy tent until my camp duties were behind me. I went to light my stove, something I had done many times before, and came up empty. You've got to be kidding me, I thought. Here I am ready to collapse, shivering, borderline hypothermic, and my stove's igniter is dead. No worries, I always carry backup fire starting tools. All of it was soaking wet. That day was so windy and rainy that water found its way into just about everything in every pack. I salvaged some of my waterproof matches but I had nothing dry to strike them against. After 30 minutes of frantic attempts, I was losing heart. Finally, I paused, took a deep breath and tried to view this all as part of my lesson in patience. I tried one more time, very carefully, and finally got one small spark to ignite the stove and soon downed 2 huge containers of tasteless hot water. It was amazing and I was grateful. Later, in my tent I thought about how these simple little lessons can be so easily overlooked if we aren't living with our minds open and clear. Without living mindfully, we not only miss the lessons but we miss the opportunity to fully appreciate the little things we have and experience in our daily lives. These little things can mean so much under extreme circumstances, but under normal everyday circumstances, they are often ignored. I would never take warm water, or warm anything else for that matter, for granted again.

That night turned out to be one of my more difficult nights in Iceland. My bivy tent is only a bit larger than my body, which is great for maintaining a comfortable inside temperature, but very bad for shifting, stretching and massaging my tightening leg muscles. There is no room to sit upright. I would have to leave the tent to do a proper stretch. This wasn't going to happen in a 35-degree rainstorm. Especially after changing into my second set of currently dry clothes. I had to come up with creative ways of rubbing my quads, calves and feet. It would have been a funny sight for a fly on the wall. At one point, I was using my right heel to massage my left calf muscle. I must have looked like a giant cricket making music. Hey, whatever it took. Eventually I fell asleep but that didn't last long. Nature called but there was no way in hell I was going outside. I'd be soaked in 5 seconds and would once again risk hypothermia. I pulled out one of my collapsible water bottles and got creative. I christened it my Iceland pee bottle and marked it with an X to avoid confusing it with my freshwater bottle. That would be one mistake I would not want to make.

Soon after my urination calisthenics, I made it back to sleep, but once again, not for very long. As previously mentioned, some Allergic Asthma sufferers are also impacted during and soon after aerobic exercise. This is called Exercise-Induced Asthma and the effects are similar to a typical Asthma incident. Some people experience symptoms (shortness of breath, chest tightness, coughing, etc.) while exercising and these symptoms worsen within 5 to 30 minutes of stopping. Although I have been challenged by this, I tend to experience what is often called "late phase" symptoms which are less severe, begin 5 hours or so after stopping, and can last for 8 to 12 hours. This wreaks havoc on my recovery while training and tripping. So there I am, exhausted, laying there trying to sleep, body aching, head pounding, wet and cold and then it begins. That big, beautiful elephant sitting down upon my chest at the worst possible time. Here was my typical thought process. Now mind you, this all moves through my brain in about 3 seconds. If not addressed properly, it's all downhill from there.

"This can't happen. I need good sleep to be able to ride standing up all day tomorrow, and the day after that, and the day after that. This could ruin my entire trip. Even worse, I could have a full-on Asthma attack in, of all places, a primitive campsite in Iceland. Alone. I could die. Wow, death. How long would it take for people to find me? Should I hit the Search and Rescue button on my SPOT satellite transmitter now? Is this really it? No, I can take a couple of hits from my rescue inhaler. Well, that always jacks up my already elevated heart rate. That'll make things worse. Oh boy, this is bad. Real bad. No good options. I'll bet my blood sugar is dropping too. I shouldn't have had that extra cup of coffee. Maybe it's the chocolate. Did I drink enough water? Am I dehydrated too? Shit. I'm gonna die."

I've learned from experience that although my symptoms are very real and medication may be required, they can be worsened or improved by using my mind. Our minds are very powerful tools. When our thoughts control us, especially at times like this, our untrained mind can make us sicker. We can control our minds by simply observing our thoughts. Just seeing our thoughts for what they are, can help dilute and dissolve their negative impact on our physical bodies. I used to get caught up in the chatter, whenever I'd have a breathing incident. Especially when off riding and camping alone somewhere. Now, I watch my thoughts and I focus on my breath. My inbreath, followed by my outbreath. In and out. I don't change the breath, I just observe it. Again, this form of mindfulness meditation has saved me on many occasions.

I had set my alarm for 6am but awoke at 5am and decided to get going but not before shaking off the shivers. In hindsight, my ultralight emergency sack vs. a large, traditional sleeping bag, wasn't the best choice of gear for an Iceland adventure. The sack packs small and is excellent at reflecting body heat back onto you when snuggled up inside but if you're not careful and do not vent the excess heat outward, you wake up wet with sweat. Seasoned campers know a wet body on a cold, windy morning is not the wisest way to start your day. However, if you vent the bag too much, you freeze. It's a tricky balance to maintain while coasting through dreamland.

After cooking up some hot water and cereal, to warm my insides, I tore down camp and rolled back into town to pick up lunch supplies for the day. At 6am there weren't many options but I made it work. Navigating irregular cobblestone paths and walkways so early in the morning helped to wake me up. No caffeine required. I still hadn't decided where I would land that next night, but my intuition told me to continue heading north toward the Snaefellsjokull volcano. I backtracked out of town, passed my campsite from the night before, and rolled on.

Most of that morning would turn out to be beautiful. Not easy by far, but absolutely gorgeous. It had everything. The sun was bright, the skies were clear and the mist broke apart then disappeared entirely. There were calm breezes and huge rainbows. I felt as if I had stepped back in time, into an ancient Icelandic fairy tale. But about 20 miles in, Iceland once again reminded me what tolerance and fortitude was all about. The cold wind and rain were back. This time the wind was focused mostly on my chest and face. It was the mother of all headwinds. Soon, every pedal stroke would be almost entirely neutralized by Mother Nature and I would struggle to keep my forward momentum. I could not coast at all. When I tried, the wind would immediately halt my progress. This brutal tug of war kept up for another 3 hours. It was zapping my energy and raising my heart rate. My breathing was borderline but I had no time to care. This was turning into a long day and I needed to keep pace to earn my rest and food at a decent hour. In between the buckets of rain, I was able to spot a camp area on my map called Breidablik, which sat another hour ahead. If I continued on, without stopping, I knew I could fight through the wind then kick back, logging a respectable 40 miles for the day.

I put all my energy into maintaining balance, moving my legs, and visualizing that camping area and expecting a particular outcome. This was a mistake. You cannot become too attached to any destination on a trip like this. There is little to no planning, so you have to be ready for anything. There are no guarantees and in Iceland, as I said before, it's clear you're on your own. I approached what appeared to be Breidablik, with no camp in sight. I pulled off for a moment next to an old abandoned building to shelter from the cutting elements, and to read an old sign leaning against the broken concrete left side wall. This building had been a part of the old camping area now defunct, dilapidated and flooded with chilled water and thick mud. The weather was getting worse and it was getting late. I couldn't stay put, but I had given my all just to get to that location, completely convinced it would be my home for the night. It wasn't meant to be. There were more tests, lessons and rewards awaiting me further down my path. It was time to visit that deep, altered state that all endurance athletes frequent.

Life, athletic events, and other adventures all require us to "do the dig" from time to time. To dig down deep to the very core of who we are and what we're made of. To use our minds and bodies in ways we could not possibly imagine under normal circumstances. That afternoon was one of my digs. I truly had nothing left. The Adventure Way mentality is fun when the going is easy but when you have to really dig without any definitive goal or destination on a map, it can be excruciating. For once again in my life, I began to focus on one mile at a time. On one breath at a time. There was nothing else to focus on. I was living life, on that standing cycle, in the present moment because there was no other moment to consider. My heart rate was redlining, my chest was tightening, and my legs were seizing. I watched this all, as a bird watcher would observe a feathered friend. I just watched. Without judgment. It's as if someone else was doing the doing and I was just a spectator. I wasn't tuning out or disassociating as you might assume. I knew exactly what was happening. I just let it be. At mile 51 of the day's total 58, I would break my own personal record for cycling standing up loaded with touring gear. I watched myself wonder if I could actually do this, then just kept going and going. I brought my ever developing contemplative tendencies into that dynamic space. This would become a moving meditation meets athletic pep (self) talk. "Keep going for the sake of going, without attachment to destination. Focus on each breath, each pedal rotation. Not zoning out. Being clear and aware of everything. Full awareness of the bicycle, the breeze, the pain, even all the fearful thoughts. Recognize them, watch them move, but do not react to them. They are not me."

Soon I found myself chatting up the local livestock along the roadway. Luckily, not one responded. As the day progressed I settled more and more into my own mind and natural rhythm. I was feeling many things, all melded together and just continued to watch these feelings, and kept on pedaling; pain, peace, fear, joy, awe, exhaustion, wakefulness, balance. I was so alone but was beginning to feel embraced by the entirety and essence of Iceland which felt much like the cool, homey mist that often surrounded and protected me in Ireland. As my body explored this strange Viking land, my mind wandered through thoughts of home and what that really meant to me and everyone else. Is home one brick and mortar corner of the universe or is the universe itself our true home? Are we local or global residents? For me, motion was always my easy chair and all the people and places I would connect with became my living television programs. My journey through Iceland was twisting me, putting that sentiment to the test. Through all the isolation and challenges I would face, would I still feel that way by the end of the trip? Would this excruciating motion still feel more like home than my real home back in Pennsylvania?

One hour later I rolled into a small settlement only to find no legal camping opportunities. I was having trouble walking, thinking and speaking and utterly lacked the gumption to negotiate with locals for squat space. I rolled on. The route was barren for the next twenty minutes and my attention to paying attention waned. Just then I spotted what looked like a disheveled farm. It was an off-the-beaten-path Icelandic Inn. It clearly couldn't host many tourists but it was open now and ready to accept this weary traveler. It turned out to be my base camp for those next two evenings.

I hadn't had the opportunity to speak to many people over those last few days. As I rolled up to the front door, I planned my words carefully. I was ready to collapse and couldn't waste any time recovering from misunderstandings. I was now shivering uncontrollably, surely a precursor to hypothermia, I thought. I needed to get out of my wet clothes and get near a fire, fast. I left my bike outside leaning against the building, carefully locked the front wheel to the frame, and brought my more valuable gear bags inside, for security reasons. It's what I would have done back home. This was, of course, a joke here in Iceland. I doubt the cows had any interest in stealing my seatless rig packed with stinky wet clothes.

When I first approached the Innkeeper I opened my mouth but nothing came out. Then, after what felt like minutes, the sound arrived. I think if I recall correctly, it was some kind of growl. Nothing intelligible. My host was polite and walked me through the registration process with his own great patience and diligence. Before I knew it, I was carrying my bike and all my gear to an easily accessible guest room. It was about the size of a large walk-in closet back in the states. There was no phone or television and that was just fine by me. I had been riding and sleeping in cold, wet clothes for days. The hot shower nestled in the corner of that same room was all I needed. I didn't even care about the bed, but I would surely utilize it just the same.

After showering, I fell back onto the mattress which sat only 2 feet from the shower stall and stared across the tiny room into a large wall mirror. It was the first time I had seen myself since arriving in Iceland. I couldn't believe my eyes. I thought, who is that guy? Is that really me? I had a huge bruise on my inner thigh from a fall the day before. My face was swollen and burned from the exertion and wind, and my lips were cracked and bloody. A scruffy beard had grown in, adding to my unsettled, mountain man look. Was this vagrant in the mirror really me? Who was "me" anyway? Was I a struggling "Asthmatic", an endurance athlete, a Project Manager, a friend, a coach, a lover, a son, a Standing Cyclist, a winner, a loser? So many things. What was the real deal or ultimate truth?

At some point, of course, we all reflect on this "Who am I?" thing. I wasn't breaking any new ground here but most do not have the chance to reflect on this question under these circumstances. I saw it as a unique opportunity. A real gift, and I knew I'd have plenty more time, alone with myself on this trip, to consider the answer. This was more than a bike trip, just as Ireland had proven to be. As before, this was more of a pilgrimage than simply an adventure or athletic endeavor. I wasn't just tearing muscles through lava fields and barren roadways. I was exploring myself, and deep inside I knew if I could do so with an open mind and heart, I would be changed forever. This notion reminded me of Sean back in Ireland and his insightful, enlightening words of wisdom.

My bike had needed some work for several days now. The near constant wet weather took its toll on all unsealed, normally lubricated parts. Also, my wheels were bent a bit and needed truing. After making the necessary adjustments, I dressed and headed down to grab some dinner and mingle with whatever locals and tourists I could find. Again, I had hoped I could speak with some degree of intelligence.

My mind wandered as I sat waiting for the server to greet me. I recalled those stories spread around about me back in Ireland. I was now envisioning locals repeating my Iceland tale, after my departure, and how bizarre it might sound. "I met this crazy American. He was bruised and bloody, walked with a limp, he couldn't speak and he rode a bicycle without a seat." It was not exactly Ireland, but this trip did have its own charm. This land and its people were very special in their own way. I learned this more each day, mostly through sheer osmosis while moving through the land, rather than by frequenting pubs as I did in Ireland. It was less of a people thing here and more of an energy thing. In fact, I later learned that my relatively unplanned destination (the Snaefellsnes Peninsula) was thought to be an important, rejuvenating region stocked with mystical elves and laced with unseen energy grids and vortexes.

Dinner rocked! That's simply the best way to put it. One of the best meals of my life. Marinated trout for starters followed by a huge hunk of Icelandic cod which melted apart in my mouth with ease. My one glass of wine went right to my head. On trips like these, there's nothing better than a meal like that, at the end of a challenging day. As it turned out, there was no one to talk to so my worries about speaking well were a waste of valuable energy. No tourists, and the locals and servers took little interest in me, my trip and my stand-up riding style. I took the time to reflect on how we often see ourselves at the center of the universe. Iceland was a humbling experience, in that particular respect. To the locals, I could be there or not. I could be hurt or healthy. It didn't really matter. In this remote land, all is as it is. You felt way out there on your own, because you were. You were not at the center of everything or anything for that matter. That reminded me how close I was to Snaefellsjokull, the great volcano made famous in the Jules Verne book, and later in several Hollywood movies, called *Journey to the Center of the Earth*. I recalled reading the story as a child and that brought warmth to my heart that evening. I believe that warmth inspired my legs to continue in that particular direction. My eleventh hour spontaneous game plan was set. That next morning, I would move closer to the 1400 meter mound, crossing the magical Snaefellsnes Peninsula in the process. At least I hoped I would.

That night did not pass easy. Before bed, my left ear began to ache and soon the annoyance turned to pain. Serious pain. This was not good. Riding standing up requires near perfect balance, virtually 100% of the time, especially in high winds. I was now having trouble walking in a straight line. When I finally fell asleep, my late phase Asthma symptoms kicked in but they were worse than usual. My normal meditative techniques were not working very well. I held my inhaler in my hand all night long, just in case. In the morning I came to realize what I was too exhausted to recognize the night before. I had been sleeping under a down comforter which triggered my allergies which worsened my symptoms. I had made a rookie Asthma Management mistake. I should have checked the tags, as I normally would, but fatigue had made me careless and mindless. My big day up and over the significant pass, which lay between me and the north shore of Snaefellsnes, had now been jeopardized. This was an all-in challenge and I needed to be well rested and strong to pull it off. I needed to be at least 50% recovered to complete this attempt, loaded with gear, out and back in one day. I was not. It was time to regroup and make some adjustments. I decided to stay checked in at the Inn one more night. I would leave all nonessentials in my room and make the big, standing push over the hill, with a lighter load. This would hopefully improve my chances of success given my exhaustion, physical pain and now serious breathing issues.

As I geared up, I realized that my breathing had distracted me from another detail. One, particularly important for riding standing up. I could not feel my right hand. It worked, sort of, but it was very numb. Riding the way I ride, my two hands and two feet are my only contact points with the bike. Take one out of the mix and the risk of falling off the road or into the path of a passing truck, increases. No fear, right? I must admit I considered aborting the attempt. It pains me to say I actually considered hanging out at the Inn, drinking the one brand of Icelandic beer they had, and just sleeping it all off. The alcohol, the pain and the exhaustion. All of it. After breakfast, I took a short walk outside, reflecting and praying along the way. I suppose I was seeking some otherworldly direction. Intuitively, what felt right? This became clear. Ride. Stand up and ride toward the volcano. Ride over the peninsula and don't stop until you reach the ocean. I could see Snaefellsjokull far in the distance, behind the Inn, peeking through the clouds in approval.

You can never take yourself too seriously. Just when you think you're the shit, something ridiculous happens to remind you what a nozzle you really are. That was me during and after breakfast. I was mentally ready to roll out and even felt confident and boastful about what I was about to do. I tried to talk about it to whomever I ran into that morning. It's like I needed that fuel, that energy back from them. The ego feed. Few were interested but they all looked at me curiously, like there was something wrong with my appearance.

I finally returned to my room to find a tissue sticking way out of my bad ear. I used it earlier that morning to clean up but must have unknowingly left one large piece stuck in place. When I went to pull it out, the tissue ripped in two leaving one fluffy chunk deep inside my ear. I had to laugh. I was running late and didn't need this bizarre distraction. I didn't want to leave it in there, for fear of infection. I couldn't get it out with my fingers. Think, think. I needed a fast solution. Just then, I recalled my friend Kathy repurposing and adhering someone's maxi pads to my arms and legs to stop the bleeding after a serious mountain bike crash in West Virginia a decade before. Sure, that sounds funny now but at the time...okay, it was still funny. Really funny. Channeling Kathy's MacGyver spirit, I opened up my tool kit and pulled out my multi-tool. It included a small set of pliers which I began to maneuver around the inside of my ear. I used the large wall mirror to guide my efforts. I couldn't stop laughing which only made things worse. I'm in Iceland, alone, with a bike tool jammed in my ear. A bizarre operation but after about 10 minutes of trial and error, it was a success and I was on my way. It was definitely a classic nozzle moment.

My journey over the hill and back that day, would be the pinnacle of my rolling Icelandic expedition. This ancient space, this big hunk of volcanic rock, would not make it easy. The first portion of the ride was difficult road riding on a narrow shoulder, with local truck traffic and the occasional confused, reckless tourist. The next section was a 12% grade up over the pass. Then rolling hills along the ridge ending in a steep descent down to the ocean near the little fishing village of Olafsvik. I would return back to the Inn the way I came. I would end the day just shy of 40 miles, assuming I would be successful.

For the first several hours I fought high winds from what seemed to be coming from all directions, much like previous legs of my trip, but now far more intense. Before, the winds had been difficult to work through but were at least gradual in nature. These winds were both powerful and sudden. Gusts powerful enough to throw me off course. They were forcing me to tuck down from my standing position to reduce drag, helping me to conserve energy. Unfortunately, this didn't help very much. My legs and lungs were being overworked and my heart rate monitor confirmed it. My average heart rate was 50% higher than it should have been, at that pace. Then I began my ascent. The temperature began to gradually drop as I rose in altitude and my heart rate increased even more. The terrain was mostly dirt and loose gravel making traction a challenge while standing. It takes a smooth and steady pedal stroke, with predictable downward force to not slip your rear wheel when pedaling standing up. This vigilance can be exhausting in itself. I then had my first significant mechanical issue of the entire trip. A rear derailleur malfunction threw off my pace and balance, launching me off the bike. I always bring my tools on trips along with a few key bike parts, wire (for securing broken assemblies), spare hardware and yes, of course, duct tape for just about anything. I was able to make the repair quickly, before cooling down too much.

As I reached the top of the pass, my eyes teared up as the ocean came into view, but I was not done or was I? I could turn around now, and be back at the Inn well before dinner. If I rode down to the water toward Olafsvik, it would mean another one and a half hours down and back up and over the pass. It didn't take me long to decide to descend. I made it this far, I was not going to turn around now. I wanted to hear and feel the ocean, firsthand. I wanted to breathe in the chilled ocean air. I needed to continue experiencing Iceland like a real Icelander. I suspected that meant being cold, wet, overworked and alone. I forged on.

I spent little time in the village knowing the return trip would be the more difficult undertaking and must not be delayed too long. I reflected on Snaefellsjokull which now, ironically, sat too close for me to fully view. I stood in its massive shadow and that would have to do. After a brief reflection on my life, this amazing adventure and my ever sharpening perception of "reality" near the water's edge, I turned my attention to ascending the big hill which loomed behind me. The hill I had glided down moments before. Soon after setting off, I experienced something very special. In my entire time in Iceland I had never truly felt a strong tailwind. Halfway up that hill the wind suddenly changed direction just long enough to propel me almost effortlessly back up through the pass. In my compromised state, I thought of my dad helping me along. I thought about a higher power, guardian angels and even Icelandic elves. I felt as if they were all at my side and had my back. A magical notion, if nothing else.

Wake up! Pay attention! Never get too comfortable. Halfway over the pass that friendly wind turned to fiend and I was suddenly launched off the bike, off the road, and down into a ditch. Yet another teachable moment. Bruised a bit, I picked myself and my bike back up and struggled to roll off during small breaks in the wind. I would get going again and ride along for another few minutes only to find myself back in the ditch. I later estimated wind speed, with the help of locals, in excess of 50 mph. Upon cresting the highest most point of the hill, I began my 5-mile descent. This brought with it new hazards. I configured this bike with rear brakes only. Coasting down the steep hill, in the high crosswinds, had me leaning heavy on my brakes to safely throttle back my speed. The pads were heating up and crumbling apart. I was concerned they would disintegrate before I reached the bottom. This continued for almost two hours until I was able to get down off the hill and back to the main roadway. By then, I was utterly spent. My legs and arms were in pain and felt as heavy as concrete, and I still had over two hours of rolling hills and standing cycling ahead of me, before I reached the Inn.

The long downhill in the cold rain chilled me to the bone. It was time to crank up my output and generate some much needed body heat. As I settled in and dug down, I couldn't help notice the quaint family farms set back deep along the roadway. I didn't see any power or telephone lines but it did seem like each one had their own little backyard waterfall. I would come to learn that Icelanders were innovative people who took full advantage of the natural hydroelectric and geothermal benefits of their island for their power and heat. These settlements were, for the most part, self-contained. This impressed and delighted me but I did wonder about the isolation, especially in the cold, wet winter months. Many of these homes were separated by hours, not minutes. My mind continued to wander and wonder. Did they home school their children? Did they socialize on the weekends? How did they communicate? I didn't even see any mailboxes. They must have quite a family unit to survive, I thought. I was humbled and moved by what I was learning in this robust land. Facts and lessons about our miraculous Earth and all the strong, stoic people who call this rock their home.

I ended my day, back at the Inn, around dinner time. At 38 miles, it wasn't my longest day but it was one of my most meaningful, in many ways. I had pressed myself and returned a more insightful person. Iceland had broken me then built me back up again. This experience set up the shot for my Lake Champlain ride, which was yet to be envisioned. That trip would be more about others than myself. A first for me. I could not have done Lake Champ without first suffering and growing through my Ireland and Icelandic adventures.

I once again ended my day with some spectacular Icelandic cod, redfish and of course a well-deserved beer (or two). Crashing back in my room, I thought about home, how my body had deteriorated, and for the first time on this trip I considered my flight schedule back to the United States. The hobo in me had no interest in such a topic but I had commitments to fulfill back home. I had a lot of ground to cover, to get back to Keflavik, and simply could not miss my scheduled flight. This trip had inadvertently developed into an out-and-back rather than a loop, so backtracking shouldn't be too unpredictable, I thought, but that didn't mean I could coast so to speak. I still had to hustle. I had a big 58 miler that following day. A leg that truly kicked my ass the first time around. Would I make it? I had no choice, I had a plane to catch. Time to dig, again.

I woke that next morning with what I sometimes call my Asthma hangover. It follows a sleep impaired evening of labored breathing, usually tied to my late phase Exercise-Induced Asthma symptoms plaguing me most of the night. It feels a little like jet lag with some residual fear of perishing alone in a foreign country thrown into the mix. Unfortunately, aspirin does little to ease these aftereffects. After pulling myself and my gear together, I went downstairs to begin my checkout routine. My host was a unique looking man who wore a huge top hat and spoke broken English. He had long scruffy hair and a silly smile. When he saw me approach, he jumped to announce that the weather today would be, you guessed it, cold, windy and rainy. He also took great care in predicting the 40+ mph headwinds expected to work against me, on my return trip to Borganes. We chatted about my previous day's accomplishment up and over Snaefellsnes Peninsula to the Olafsvik region. I told him about the high winds I encountered and how it repeatedly threw me off my rig. He laughed, patted me on the back and told me how lucky I had been. He explained that almost every day automobiles are blown off that road and down into the gully. I had apparently ridden on a calm day.

My 58 miles back to Borganes were predictable. Of course, gut wrenching but still relatively uneventful. I did experience a couple of mechanical issues, pulled a back muscle, and met another bicycle tourist. He was from a small town outside of Venice, Italy. He kept staring at where my seat was supposed to be. He was too polite to ask and I was too tired to speak. There were moments on this particular leg when I considered just bagging it all and hitching a ride directly to the airport. I had made it up north. Far enough for me. Pretty cool. I could go home now, why wait? But this trip wasn't about a goal, it was about the direct experience of it all. It was about Asthma Management, surviving and thriving, and whenever possible, sharing. It was about the challenges, self-discovery and, most of all, practicing patience. It was never about the end game. You can always go farther or faster. Someone is always going to be better than you at something, at some point. Why should any of that matter? I probably could have squeezed out another mile or two on any given day or pedaled a little faster. When is enough, enough? You just know, deep down inside. You reach a point in life, deep within your mind and soul, when you know when to stop and that it's okay to stop. A deep sense of peace comes and all is right with the world. Not a sermon on the virtues of competition, I'll give you that, but my journey and these passages have little to do with competition and more to do with a growing wakefulness.

Back to the material world. I pulled over to stretch after rolling into town and realized my legs actually hurt to the touch. A first for me. I was walking like John Wayne and could have sworn that I was bleeding from my eyes. I semi-collapsed on a curb near a small dessert shop. My mind was buzzing so I decided to practice a brief calming meditation. Thoughts came and went, and I let them be, without judgment. My heart slowed, my breathing improved and my head cleared. I began to laugh out loud. I laughed at my body, my pain, and my bizarre seatless bicycle. I laughed at my own ego and how it had atrophied a bit from lack of attention. I reflected on peace, appreciation, optimism and unconditional love. Show it, mean it, no agenda. Family. Friends. I reflected upon my silly, angry arm injury from back home, which followed me relentlessly, simmering on the back burner, over these many miles. The aching arm and shoulder caused by my own mindless intolerance. Had I learned anything, I questioned. I truly felt I had. At least beginning to. I was looking forward to returning home, to continue my practice. To prove it.

That night I made camp outside of town. After cooking and completing camp chores, I sat looking up at the late day sky. I prayed for some sunlight through those cloudy skies. Moments later, for what seemed like the first time in days, the clouds drifted apart just for a minute or so and I basked in the glow of that bright white Icelandic sun, with great appreciation for the divine coincidence. Another special Icelandic moment. A place in space and time that stays with me to this day, to some degree, running in the background like an anti-virus computer program keeping my soul and gray matter safe and healthy. I had fully embraced the unknown. For at least a while, all fear and discomfort had left me. My lungs and chest were light, my mind was calm and my heart cracked open a little more. I felt empowered, balanced and complete.

The remainder of my time in volcanic Iceland was a true tale of trains, planes and automobiles. After riding back to Reykjavik, the same way I had traveled out, I responsibly disposed of my remaining camp stove fuel at that same campground in the center of the city, and settled there for the night. I rose early and cycled my way back to the bus station where I had locked up my bike box. I dismantled my rig and packed it up for the 45-minute shuttle bus ride down to Keflavik airport. Before settling into my airline seat for a nap, I pulled out my dad's old black leather keychain that I always travel and cycle with. I wondered if he was with me and what he thought of my accomplishment. He was a simple, insightful, quiet man. I suspect he wouldn't have understood my standing cycling. Not entirely anyway. He would have, however, understood the value of my lessons. What a trip. What a life.

*The early days, riding traditional
mountain bikes in Moab, UT*

*Kathy, Jim, me, and Bob kicking off near the Canadian
border – Montana Great Divide Trip 2005.*

Another long ascent, recumbent touring off-road along the GDMBR.

Endless logging roads and beautiful scenery
in Grizzly Bear country in northern Montana.

Classic Montana wilderness,
as viewed from two-wheels.

I took this trailside sign very seriously...

Jim and me, laid back in Montana.
Is it beer o'clock yet?

Friendship and teamwork in action.

After descending "the" technical GDMBR section – the
Recumbent is still in one piece. Me, not so sure.

An ancient Irish burial ground.
Surprisingly welcoming.

A magical view of the Inch shoreline
in southwestern Ireland.

Israeli tourists near Inch beach,
trying out my seatless ride.

Cold and wet outside of Tralee, Ireland.

An end of day single-track treat in Iceland.

*A typically confusing road sign found
along rural Icelandic roadways.*

*The famous Snaefellsjokull volcano, in Iceland,
from the book and movies called
Journey to the Center of the Earth.*

*Chillin' in Iceland with Helen Thayer's desert adventure book called,
Walking the Gobi.*

*A storm rolling in on my primitive
campsite in southwest Iceland.*

*Riding through Reykjavik, Iceland
well before sunrise.*

*Stand-up touring through Icelandic
lava fields.*

*Staging gear in Burlington, VT before starting
my Lake Champlain Stand Up To Cancer tour.*

*A sneak peek at what's under the
foam padding — a cutoff seat-tube.*

*En route to Chambly, Canada on the
Lake Champlain SU2C tour.*

Stand-up cycling through Plattsburgh, N.Y.
city streets, courtesy of FOX TV.

Bikepacking with "The Creature from the Black Lagoon."
A long night filled with bizarre sounds.

A colder than expected morning in the
Adirondack Mountain foothills.

An unusual seatless silhouette in Vermont.

*Fixed-gear Standing Cyclist touring near McKeesport, PA
at the start of the Mesothelioma Challenge.*

*Threading the needle. Mindful stand-up pedaling
outside of Pittsburgh, PA.*

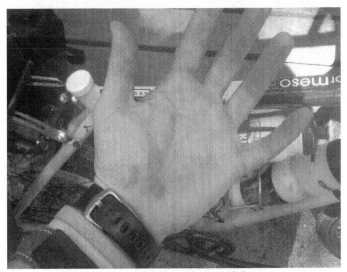

*Let the blisters begin – only several days into
The Mesothelioma Challenge.*

North meets south along the Great Alleghany Passage.

Navigating the spooky Paw Paw tunnel, 4 days into the Mesothelioma Challenge.

*A typical early morning scene along the
Great Alleghany Passage.*

*Myself, Larry Davis, and Courtney Davis wrapping
up the Mesothelioma Challenge in Washington, D.C.*

Larry Davis running alongside me, into D.C.

Chapter 7 - LAKE CHAMPLAIN

Upon returning to Pennsylvania, I had to regroup before immediately entering back into life as I knew it. I took a day with loved ones to share my Iceland trip journal and get my brain around the physical accomplishment. I had been reflecting, along the way, on heart and mind experiences and growth opportunities but it wasn't until I returned home and updated my, then, Asthma Management-theme website that I truly grasped the physicality of what I had done. I had cycled 33 hours without sitting down, in 6 consecutive days of touring on and off road, for a total of 234 miles. I averaged 5.4 hours of actual standing ride time per day and burned a total of 21,590 kcal in the process. My average daily miles came in at 39, with several days exceeding 55 miles. I thought my post-trip recovery would take weeks, but it actually took about 3 months for my body to fully recover. It was the most grueling activity I had ever undertaken, up to that point, and the most rewarding by far.

While recovering, I decided to poke around the internet to see if anyone else was doing this sort of thing. If there was, I couldn't find them. Was I really the only one in the world training and touring standing up? What did it matter, anyway? I was doing this for myself. It was my way of getting back on the bike after Asthma. But this trip had changed my way of thinking, just as Ireland had. I was changing as a person. I wanted to continue my standing cycling for my health and fitness, but I couldn't help recall how popular I had become in Ireland. I started thinking about merging passion and purpose. I broke it all down, in my head. I loved riding this way. It was challenging but oddly comfortable, for me anyway. It was fresh and fun. My mind and body worked well with this style of training and touring. I considered all the people who engaged with me simply because of how I was touring. It gave me the ability to connect with people who otherwise wouldn't have given me a second glance. Riding without a seat certainly brought attention to me and what I was doing, whether I liked it or not. Finally, throw in my Iceland isolation, ego-assessment, and big picture lessons. I felt the need to pull this all together. To challenge myself doing something I loved to do, while contributing or serving in some meaningful way.

For the next several months I researched ways in which I could connect my interests with a greater purpose. Something beyond myself. This eventually led me to Stand Up To Cancer. SU2C was a newly introduced non-profit initiative founded by well-known television producer and Cancer survivor, the now late Laura Gaskin. It was backed by the entertainment industry and didn't seem to need any help from a lone riding oddity from rural Pennsylvania, but I was compelled just the same. I appreciated their approach. They used donation money to form and manage Dream Teams of doctors and scientists all dedicated to finding a cause and improving treatment programs for many forms of Cancer. The

Project Manager in me connected with this logical, team methodology. It was all about pooling specialized resources and encouraged sharing ideas rather than keeping theories and clinical testing secret to protect the ambitions of the research community. Cancer was not about competition, I thought. I could relate to that. It was about collaboration, compassion and creatively, or at least I thought it should be. It appeared I had found the direction I was looking for, and the common stand up theme was a perfect fit. I would ride for SU2C. My top goal was to tribute the group, help raise awareness for the cause and the way SU2C goes about supporting it. I figured if I raised any money, that would be icing on the cake.

By that time, many of my close friends and family had been touched by Cancer in some way or another. As I've mentioned before, my mother herself is a Cancer survivor. I had lost many relatives to Cancer, and several close friends were actually working through Cancer at the time of my trip. This further fueled my intentions to craft a Standing Cyclist solo tour based around Stand Up To Cancer. I had the why already, so I started brainstorming the when, where, and how of it all. My trip research led me to several fly-away locations in the U.S. but money was tight so a drivable destination seemed more feasible. I spent many hours chatting about this with friends, and also considered my many options during numerous miles of moving meditation on the bike.

I eventually decided to ride the Lake Champlain Bikeway. It was a 360 mile on-road route around Lake Champlain. It would lead me through New York, Vermont and into Canada. I would ride the classic route standing up loaded with gear, without a seat, and would camp whenever possible to remain close to my natural surroundings. I would schedule it for the 400th Anniversary of the lake, which I thought would help draw attention to my cause.

I was beginning to learn how to organize, market and promote an event. This trip was a great classroom in which to learn and develop these skills. This was 2009 and social media was now playing-in heavily to adventure travel and fundraising. I was all over that, as well. I had to be. This trip was different, so my attitude toward seemingly unnecessary hubbub had to change. No flying under the radar, before, during or after my trip. What I was attempting needed to be front and center at all times. I didn't care much for this mindset but I knew it was a necessary evil. I knew I needed to keep a close eye on the attention and always remember that it was all about the cause I was supporting, and not about feeding my identity and fueling my small self. This was, of course, tough at times. When you want people to know about your project and your project revolves around you and what you do, you must at times self-promote. I never could stand this and still can't. I long for the day when I can delegate this uncomfortable chore entirely to others. Funny how times change. As a young man, I never had trouble with that kind of self-promotion. Especially in local pubs on a Friday night.

My outer trip purpose was settled but my inner, subtler theme was not yet apparent. The days and weeks leading up to my departure would foreshadow my future trip teachings but I was too manic with last minute action items to catch those hints. In between building my Lake Champ adventure cycle, training, working, helping with home duties and gearing up, I was missing the bigger picture. I was getting stuck in my own self-imposed hamster wheel existence, as we so often do when a grander goal lies before us. As a trip theme, balance was slowly creeping its way to the top of my short list of possibilities. Balanced thinking and balanced action.

This would be my longest Standing Cyclist trip yet and I needed the right tool for the job. To increase efficiency and minimize rolling resistance, I had considered a modified road touring bicycle but after reviewing my route, I was concerned that long standing days on dirt and rock shoulders would break parts and blow tires. 29er mountain bikes were becoming popular at the time and caught my eye for this trip. Large diameter tires roll easier over mixed, uneven terrain and those frame geometries were close to what felt best to me in my standing position. I started sketching out tube lengths, angles and a wheelbase that showed promise, based on my previous trip bikes. After finding the right mix, I began to experiment by modifying some old frames and switching out buckets of parts, until I landed at a combination that would serve me well.

Next, I needed to find a production frame designed for 29 inch wheels with wide tires, front and rear touring racks, plenty of water bottle cages and it needed to be steel. For long distance tours, steel has always been my favorite frame material. A cracked frame made from steel can be easily welded and repaired, even in remote areas of the world. Steel frames are typically less costly, as well, which at that time was a major factor for me. I was self-sponsored and needed to cut costs wherever possible. It didn't take long to decide on the newly introduced Salsa Fargo expedition touring frame. It was perfect for what I had in mind and the frame geometry came very close to matching my standing specs.

I took a day off from work and made the 4-hour trip to State College, PA and back, to purchase a new Fargo frame from a local bike shop. I got some funny looks when I explained to them what I was planning to do with this new 29er. As I have often experienced, they thought I was kidding around until I gave them one of my cards which led them to my (Team) Standing Cyclist website. After that, they simply thought I was out of my mind to even consider attempting Lake Champ, standing up the whole way. As before, prior to previous trips, a small part of me was in agreement.

The date was set. I would leave PA on September 13th, 2009 and set up my Burlington, VT base camp at the Champlain Inn, a motel just outside the center of town. It was small, inexpensive, clean and was right across the street from a coffee shop. That wasn't the best part. After discovering what I was attempting they had agreed to let me leave my car in their already tight lot for the duration of my Lake Champ ride. A huge win. One less thing to worry about while tuning up my gear, body and emotions.

Before hitting the sack, the night before beginning my ride, I walked into the center of Burlington for a steak and a beer, potentially my last real dinner for the next 8 days. I ate every morsel and drank every sip with full attention and apprecia-tion. It was truly outstanding. I was sitting outside, at a sidewalk table, in a huge open courtyard closed to traffic. I was surrounded by what seemed to be hundreds of diners and partygoers. I wondered how many were battling Cancer. I wanted to stand up tall on my chair and announce my in-tentions. I wanted everyone to know what I was about to do, but I was afraid. Would anyone really care? Will anyone really care, when I'm done, assuming of course I can actually finish the ride. I didn't know for sure. I was conflicted about many things. I could be just wasting my time, risking my own safety and health, for no good reason. How would I promote my trip, to raise awareness for Stand Up To Cancer, when I doubted my own ability and when I preferred to fly under the radar rather than shout from the rooftops. I would soon learn that a balanced approach would yield the best results, in every way.

After a quick egg sandwich and coffee fix to fuel my start, I rolled off the next morning across Burlington to Local Motion for some last minute supplies and maps. Local Motion is a small but powerful, member supported organization focused on human-powered recreation and transportation for healthy and sustainable Vermont communities. I had begun teaming with them months before when researching my Lake Champ route. They were both friendly and helpful. Stopping by their Steele St. Trailside Center was an inspiring way for me to begin my trip. I met many people there who were both curious and excited about what I was doing and more importantly, why I was doing it. This was a real confidence builder and helped launch me on my way.

My first day was textbook cyclotouring. A few mechanical issues, wonderful conversations with locals, tight shoulders, traffic, a little under-hydration, rolling hills and scattered clouds. Overall, it was outstanding. Unlike Iceland, I was exposed socially much of the day. A perfect setting for raising awareness for a good cause. I was settling in to the balance of riding for my own wellness, and someone or something else at the same time. I thought a lot about my balance theme that first day. Balancing my relatively heavy, standing cycle, balancing my thoughts and balancing my intentions and actions. I looked back on how out of balance I had become in prepping for this trip, while back home in PA. My own unique balance point had slipped off center and that had me questioning everything. Myself, my Asthma, my relationships, my work and why I was actually taking this Standing Cyclist thing to another level. Now that I was finally out alone, on the road, I could look back on all of this and that reflection was good for me. It was a valuable opportunity I would not waste.

It's a shame many of us can't or won't open up our schedule to look deeply at ourselves and our intentions under normal circumstances, before life goes sideways. Before I left home, my daily spiritual practice also suffered the side effects of a busy, uncontrolled existence. A key aspect of my life, a crucial component, and I didn't even have the time for that or rather believed I didn't. It's funny how even when we know what works and what doesn't, we often (sometimes consciously, sometimes unconsciously) choose what doesn't. I wondered why. I hoped this trip would bring me some big answers to important questions.

My first night was spent camping lakeside at Champlain Lake Campground. It was a gorgeous evening in a truly magical location. I had ridden 44 miles without sitting down, a unique accomplishment that brought with it a unique blend of exhaustion and exhilaration. My chest was tight, my breathing labored a bit and my legs were spent, but none of that mattered. I was high on the joy of this whole adventure, and it had barely begun. Overall, I felt great. How could I feel this good? Should I feel this good, I thought? For the first time on a Standing Cyclist trip, or any bike trip for that matter, I was tapping into feelings of a bigger purpose outside of myself. I found that thoughts of the cause, and of the many people I know and knew that struggled through Cancer, was giving me far more fuel than I had ever imagined. But it was much more than a simple adrenaline rush. I would even go as far as calling it spiritual in nature. Everything was falling into place, finally. I was doing what I loved, for the right reasons, and I was thrilled about the correctness of it all. I felt truly in-flow. I drifted off to sleep nestled in my favorite old bivy tent listening to potent opera music seeping through a neighboring tent wall. Not my first choice for a lullaby but I fell into it just fine.

Earlier in 2009, I began studying marathon and ultramarathon runners. These elite endurance athletes fascinated me. I was curious about what made them tick. Why exactly do they do what they do? Some, I found, enjoyed the rush of challenging themselves. Others were obsessed with competition and winning, but a true love for pure adventure and a sincere passion for the unknown, was almost always present. I admired these athletes and in my gut I knew I could learn much from their training routines, both physical and mental. Although lacking an outwardly competitive nature, I often challenged myself inside and always gave every athletic undertaking my all. In this area, the works of author/athletes such as Ultramarathonman Dean Karneses, *Runner's World* Magazine Guru Bart Yasso and plant-powered endurance athlete Rich Roll have helped inspire, educate and drive me forward as a Standing Cyclist.

There is a body awareness, rhythm, mental component, and physical requirement shared between running long distances and what I do. This would become more apparent as my geared, coast-able designs morphed into single speed, fixed-gear (no coasting) standing designs. On this particular trip, I chose to pack and read Bart Yasso's book, *My Life on the Run*. It was a small, stocky print copy that would hold up well to the rigors of a long distance tour. I'd open it nightly and knock out a chapter or two before dozing off. It was the perfect cap to a well worked day, and set the stage for dreams of challenge and completion.

This was my first excursion on which I used my SPOT satellite transmitter to track my daily trip progress, live. I would later program a SPOT My Adventure page to collect and map my data and photos, as part of my SU2C awareness campaign. I rode each day with the small orange SPOT device on my handlebar bag. Every 10 minutes it automatically sent my GPS coordinates, posted on a digital map, to Standing Cyclist email subscribers wishing to follow my progress. After returning home, some wannabe comedian friends would tell me they checked the live map each morning and evening, just to make sure the blip was still moving. This way they knew I was still breathing.

Day 2 led me through the Canadian countryside, where I proceeded to get myself lost, not once but twice. It was a chilly day and cloudy, but luckily there was no rain in sight. My heart rate was a little high but I attributed that to the rolling hills and my excitement entering a new country. It's always extra exciting when I leave the U.S. You never know what will happen next. I heard out on-the-road that the Auberge Harris Hotel in St. Jean-sur-Richelieu had good food and great area maps, so I set my sights on that goal, for that particular evening. My map showed an access point about 10 miles down a dirt trail but to reach the trail, which sat about 50 feet below the bridge I was riding across, I had to haul my bike loaded with panniers down a multi-tiered steel staircase. For one moment I thought about how cool it would be to ride down but realized an injury now would ruin the trip and impact the cause. The moment I began this ride, I realized it stopped being about me, only. I had to consider the bigger purpose and decided against the urban stunts and walked down with the 85 lb. rig on my shoulder. Walking down turned out to be harder than expected. Maybe even more difficult than riding the open grate structure.

I rolled into the hotel parking lot just before dark and right on time for dinner. The chef and owner, a kind woman interested in the purpose of my ride, provided me with key route details for my remaining Canadian miles, before crossing back into the United States. That was good news for me. I hadn't thought much about my next leg. She knew the crew down at Local Motion in Burlington, Vermont and was excited to hear I kicked off my journey from their doorstep.

After settling into my room, washing up and changing into my spare, (semi) clean set of clothes, I headed down for some chow. As I sat filling my belly with home cooked meat and potatoes, chased by a local brew, I thought about how I truly wanted to camp that night. I love sleeping outside, under the stars. My Asthma tends to act up in sealed up hotel rooms but the Auberge was a fine establishment with good ventilation and luckily for me, no feather comforters. I was in good hands. Also, for this trip, camp nights would work against me and my purpose. I am more isolated in primitive campground situations with less people to connect with. My success riding around Lake Champlain would be measured by how much of a buzz I could kick up for Stand Up To Cancer. I would be more effective at raising awareness for the cause in highly populated areas. Meeting local families impacted by Cancer and coordinating media efforts is certainly easier when riding through large towns and sleeping in hotels, versus bushwhacking your way down mountain trails and camping out alone. This was proving to be a difficult adjustment for me. Like many people, I have always been more comfortable in the woods than in the hustle and bustle of the city. Being close to nature helps ground me. It draws out my creativity, calms my mind and opens my heart. Ireland, and even Iceland at times (if you can believe that), placed me in populated areas but also provided enough solitude to keep me balanced. For this trip, for the sake of the cause, I would need to intentionally place myself in crowded areas. What I was doing needed to get noticed. The very opposite of what I'd typically do, while riding or at any other time for that matter.

Sitting at my cozy little dinner table, at the Auberge, I started flipping through a local Canadian newspaper to discover that Lance Armstrong had recently participated in a big benefit ride in Montreal. The story was both well written and inspiring. Lance was always on my radar. I had followed his career from before his Cancer, through his (first) comeback and well into his multiple Tour de France wins. I've never been one to idolize sports figures or entertainers but if I had, it would have been Lance that topped my list. As I sit writing this portion of my story, I am reflecting back on Oprah Winfrey's powerful interview with Lance, one month back from the time of this writing, during which he admitted to doping and the elaborate related cover-ups. I've since spent time trying to process the falsehoods and the reasons behind them, from various points of view. From his and also from those seriously impacted by the situation. My personal opinion regarding doping in sports matters little, but after the initial sting of this drama, I am left only with deep compassion for all involved, including Lance himself. No one will walk away from this clean and comfortable. For me, Livestrong, as a charitable organization, was and is far more important than any one sports figure, campaign or tagline. When I look back on what inspired me most through the Lance years, by far, it was his involvement in Livestrong and the good they do within the Cancer community.

As I continued to scan the publication, my eyes shifted from Lance to Patrick. That was the week movie star Patrick Swayze lost his long battle with Pancreatic Cancer. I was suddenly thrust back fully into what I was doing out there. Why I was riding MY tour. I tried to fully engage in the article. I wanted to put myself at the center of the challenge, alongside him and his family. To fully immerse myself in that moment when he first heard his diagnosis and learned of his chances of survival. To do this ride justice, I needed to swim in that uncertainty, fear, fight and acceptance, to some extent. I needed to revisit old feelings of lost family members and friends, who like Patrick, refused to give up but were taken just the same. I needed to feel that pain, once again, to truly appreciate their suffering and in many cases, celebrate their recovery. That naturally occurring practice of empathy and compassion turned out to be my most valuable fuel for standing up for those hundreds of miles.

My breathing and blood sugar were both issues that night in Canada. I had strange dreams filled with foreshadowing. Dreams of writing books about my adventures, perhaps using them to raise awareness for special causes. After only 6 hours of terrible sleep, I woke to a stiff neck, aching core, and painful hands and wrists after logging 52 hard standing miles the day before. The lengthy back-to-back, daylong, sessions were already beginning to take their toll. Without the ability to recover properly, my body would continue to rebel. This was only the start of day 3 and I was already faltering. Doubt began to creep into my gut but I didn't show my nervousness as I rolled out of the hotel, saying my goodbyes along the way. I wasn't sure of the day's route and where I would bed down at its close. I heard rough roads were ahead and I was concerned about my wheels and tires holding up. They would not be ideal in super gnarly conditions, especially with my gear and body weight added in.

The route north along the canal to Chambly was extraordinarily beautiful. I could have excluded this northern most section from my trip but I'm happy I didn't. It's one of several route options many Lake Champlain Bikeway cyclotourists opt to avoid. After rolling into town and meeting with some local bicycle shop owners, I backtracked down to St. Jean and set my sights on the U.S. Border. It was smooth sailing until I met my first dog of the trip. Did I say dog? He was more like a pony with fangs. A big, angry gray Great Dane. I had never seen a Great Dane up close. I always thought they were kind of cute (in a giant dog sort of way) but this one was launching at me at full speed from a backyard bar-b-cue. Without time to think rationally, I jerked my body forward and began to sprint uphill loaded with gear. His head was level with my chest. The owner appeared to be angry at me for riding past their house (along a public roadway) and did little to stall the chase. As I crested the hill I glanced over to see my new friend finally slowing and heard drunken laughter in the distance.

I had to pull off the road to get my heart rate in check. It was spiking and my breathing was labored. I felt my chest tighten and knew I was close to a breathing incident. I quickly did a standing meditation to reduce my heart rate and lower my blood pressure. When my breathing was no longer an issue, I noticed a sharp pain in my left leg. My sudden launch had tweaked the muscles and tendons around my knee. Even standing in place and walking was now painful, how was I going to ride a seatless bike another 300 miles? I needed ice and I needed it fast but until I cleared U.S. customs, icing my injury would not be an option.

Five miles down the road, I rolled into customs at the U.S. Border. I was certain getting back into my home country would be simple and swift. I was wrong. One of the custom officers eyed my seatless frame suspiciously. "After 9/11 we can't be too careful," one of them said with a serious tone. It appeared that what I was doing was so unusual that they didn't buy my story. I guess they thought I was smuggling explosives, or perhaps drugs, inside my cut-off hollow seat tube. I gave them my Standing Cyclist website address. After about an hour, they came around and let me back into the U.S.A. I was home, so to speak.

I took a chance on a little lakeside hotel in Rouses Point, New York about 30 miles north of Plattsburgh, which turned out to be a great decision. The room was clean and relatively allergen-free and the scenery was rejuvenating. Blue skies and gentle warm breezes capped off a brutal 58-mile day. After settling in and icing my knee, I limped to town to buy some bagels for the next day's ride. I used it as reflection time to consider my ride along the canal near Chambly, my Great Dane, and my new buddies at U.S. Customs. I remembered a funny little man in an old pickup truck, while still in Canada, who stopped to chat with me in French. I didn't understand a thing he said but he seemed to enjoy himself, smiling and laughing, so I played along. I'll bet he was trying to tell me something important. I should have paid better attention way back in French class. The only morsel I digested was the phrase, "fare de portage," which, if I recall correctly, means "carry the boats over land." Maybe not. Well, either way, it always reminds me of the concept of following a spiritual practice of some sort to attain liberation. Once you attain it, the practice itself becomes unnecessary. Just as a boat becomes unnecessary after reaching land. There's no need to carry the boat over land, it's purpose has been fulfilled.

When I returned to the hotel, all I wanted to do was crash. I was toast but I had business to attend to. I had to update several Plattsburgh reporters who were interviewing me the following day, as I passed the Plattsburgh Chamber of Commerce. It would be a tricky balancing act. If I arrived too soon on interview day, I would cool down and my muscles would seize up, jeopardizing the rest of my riding day. If I arrived too late, I would risk missing the interviews coordinated to raise awareness for Stand Up To Cancer.

That next day, as it turned out, I rolled into town almost one hour early after hustling down from Rouses Point that morning, overexerting myself unnecessarily. I had time to kill. Okay, I would use it to eat, rehydrate myself and prep my bike for the rest of my day's ride. Not a chance. Before I knew it, I was being filmed by FOX TV reporter Courtney Davis. I broke free from my pedaling trance, to see a person standing in the middle of the road with a monster TV camera on her shoulder. It appeared to be bigger than she was but Courtney managed her camera with ease and dodged clear of my loaded bike in perfect sync with my forward motion.

Although excited about the exposure for the cause, I was secretly disappointed. I was hurting and needed to rest. It wasn't the best time for an interview. I wondered if I'd make any sense at all. My breathing was shallow and I couldn't shake the rubbery feeling in my arms and legs. I was seriously distracted but after pulling off near the Plattsburgh Chamber of Commerce, Courtney soon put me at ease and prepped me for my first Standing Cyclist interview...ever. Honestly, I was nervous and stiff during setup. I hadn't had a proper shower or worn clean clothes in days, after sweating and camping through almost 200 miles of the route. Now I've got this reporter who I've just met, up close and personal, sliding microphone wires up my shirt. When I should have been thinking about her upcoming questions, all I could think of was how bad I smelled. Again, Courtney was a trooper, dealing with my "road cologne" and guiding the interview like the pro that she is. It went well, at least her part anyway. Thank goodness for editing.

As soon as my first interview was behind me, my second was lined up and ready to go. This time Josh, a Press Republican newspaper reporter, would be asking the questions for an article covering my trip and the bigger purpose behind it. Twenty minutes and several photos later, I geared back up and headed off through Plattsburgh, swerving around grates in the road and Courtney's FOX News vehicle, which had followed me for several miles collecting additional footage along the way. After about twenty minutes, I was once again on my own, out on the open road. The pressure of the interview process was behind me and I settled back into a familiar riding rhythm. My muscles warmed and my mind focused on the breeze, the bumps, my breath and the steady spinning of my legs.

I rolled to a stop near Ausable Chasm, NY and set up camp right on the lake. It was the perfect spot with all the right feelings to go along with it. Feelings of freedom, adventure and contentment. Feelings of accomplishment. At just shy of 40 miles, I didn't ride a big day but I did help spread the word for Stand Up To Cancer, in my own little way at least. It felt good. Actually, it felt great. After setting up camp and cooking up some noodles, I sat near the water listening to Phish on my MP3 player and thought about the new friends I had made. Although I felt I had known Courtney for years, I underestimated the importance of meeting her. I couldn't have possibly predicted where our friendship would lead me. Within the coming year, she would share with me her father's ongoing battle with Mesothelioma Cancer. I would learn about Asbestos, the man-made cause of this fatal affliction which, at the time of this writing, is still legally in use within the United States and much of the world. In the coming months, I would grow to respect Larry Davis and his tireless fight to ban Asbestos and I would begin training to ride for Larry and his cause. It would be a training season and solo event I would never forget. The stars that night were extra bright and numerous. I meditated and prayed for a successful next few days then fell asleep beneath that spectacular star show with a growing sense of boundlessness and awe.

As the night progressed, the temperature dropped significantly. I had to put on my extra set of clothes and nestled up inside my lightweight foil emergency sleeping sack. It's always tough to maintain a comfortable body temp under these circumstances. First you're cold, then you're sweating, then you start to shiver. This cycle continues throughout the night, but with practice a balance point is possible. I remember lying awake at one point thinking about how fortunate I was to even have a tent and emergency sack, whenever needed. I thought about the numerous homeless people I had seen back in Burlington and in other parts of the country while on bicycle trips. Their daily challenges were far more difficult. I counted my blessings and drifted back off to sleep.

Here's a small bikepacking gem. Always count your tent stakes before you roll off. Apparently, I had missed a few the last time I had packed up my gear. Around 4:30am, a strong wind nearly ripped the rain fly off my small tent. I needed to stake it down and discovered I was missing almost half of my stakes. There I am outside in the wind, all cramped up and twisted from the previous day's ride, using rocks, twigs and my camp knife to stab down my tent into the dirt and weeds. By the time I got settled inside, I had a brutal ache in my left quad but lacked the room to massage it. I had to crawl back out to work the muscle but then the wind would loosen up the makeshift tent stakes, and the cycle continued. This went on for far too long before the weather calmed and I finally fell back to sleep. Truly, I couldn't complain. This is all part of the game. After a while, you get comfortable with this sort of discomfort and simply laugh it off.

I awoke at 6:30am to the rushing sound of lake waves tumbling onto the shore. The wind off the lake was kicking in and my tent fly was once again in jeopardy of sailing off down the dirt trail behind my campsite. I was hungry but tired and cold as well, which results in a bucket of conflicting emotions. You really feel like sleeping in. Eventually, you drag yourself out of the tent (because you have no choice) and make things happen. You address normal camp chores along with some occasional damage control. That morning, my "damage" turned out to be the mold at the bottom of one of my water bottles. When I trip, I usually carry several plastic water bottles each with their own purpose. One is just plain spring water. One is a highly concentrated mix of electrolyte powder and water. A third has a concentrated mix of water and a powdered endurance drink designed for extended periods of high output. Often, I'll include a fourth bottle on my frame, with diluted organic coconut water. As I ride standing throughout each day, I'll typically take 5 to 10 second drink breaks 3 to 5 times an hour. I'll sip from one or several bottles per break session, depending upon how I'm feeling, weather conditions, trail or road conditions, and how far along I am within my day's route. I've become used to this routine which allows me to consume the equivalent of about one oversized water bottle per ninety minutes of riding. This system has served me well for over 6 years now, on most Standing Cyclist adventures. The only problem with this system is maintenance. I have to work hard at keeping my stored powders dry and my bottles clean. Significant day/night shifts in both temperature and humidity can result in unwanted bottle slime as I've come to call it, and even mold.

A little mold here and there isn't much of an issue to most people, however, when you suffer from Allergic Asthma and you're highly sensitive to mold spores, you don't want any part of that, especially 200 miles into a 400 mile standing bike trip. I slipped up the night before and, on this particular morning, I woke to both slimy and moldy bottles, without a bottle brush (or soap) readily available and had to get creative. I ended up using a small camera tripod I was carrying, along with some hand sanitizer, to clean things up before packing up camp and rolling off around 8:30am. Four days down, four more to go.

Day 5 was full of surprises. Some pleasant, some, not so much. For those unfamiliar with New York State, particularly the Adirondack Mountains and foothills, here's a little insight. Steep hills, wind, loose road surfaces, blind corners, poor cell reception, and miles and miles of...not much. Did I mention the steep hills? The 'Dacks sport a total of 46 High Peaks all exceeding 4,000 feet in elevation, and for those next two days, I felt as if I was navigating each and every one, twice over. I've always loved the Adirondacks so this wasn't exactly torture. I had done my share of snowshoeing, hiking and even cycling in this gorgeous territory, however, I had never ridden here standing up. A challenge indeed and one I would not soon forget. I settled in for a long day, out of the saddle...without a saddle.

Riding on those isolated, tree-lined roads, I had a lot of brain time. As I often do, I used some of that time to read my body and mind. To assess where I was at, inside and out. How I was feeling and flowing. I began with my physical checklist. Feet? Pain, but the thick SmartWool socks I changed into this morning were helping a bit. Back? Feeling strong, no pinch, no ache, not much anyway. Legs? Heavy from the hills but no significant lactic acid burn. Hands? Wrists? Shoulders? Not so good today. Weakening. Will have to bump up my strength training and upper body work when I return home. Next came my mental check-up and tune-up. Sad? Joyful? Lonely? Excited? Frightened? Confident? Yes, all of the above. Time for a few small adjustments, or mind/body course corrections. Then there's my spiritual checklist as well. Do I remember why I'm out here? For whom? Am I expanding or contracting? Did I meditate today? Did I pray today? Have I expressed my gratitude, right here, right now, for having this opportunity and ability? I've come to realize that frequent, self-assessment is key when attempting extraordinary activities. It proves useful when training, making food choices, balancing work and home life, and in business. Highly conscious living, both on and off the bike.

Just as the going got tougher, and my mindful self-assessment drifted back and forth between ego and altruism, I was startled by a howling pack of people popping out of a supersized SUV as I rolled into a little Adirondack village, about 25 miles into my day. It was an amped up family that had come out to support me on my 400-mile journey around the lake. Parents, kids, even the family dog were hooting and flailing around to get my attention. "Hey stand up guy! Go, go, go! You can do it!" they shouted. This couldn't have come at a better time. I was now beginning to hurt, bad. It wasn't obvious to the outside world but inside I was overexerting, overheating and running out of steam. My legs had gotten much heavier and my upper body was fatigued and, at times, in significant pain. My ankles and feet, overtaxed by driving a loaded bicycle up steep, long hills, were now twisting and collapsing and my ample socks no longer provided enough cushion to ease the stress on my soles.

Based on what the family was shouting, it was clear they had seen the FOX television coverage from yesterday's road interview with Courtney and her crew. Perhaps the newspaper article as well. They had made it their mission to hunt me down and cheer me on. I had come to find out upon my return home, that the TV and print coverage reached tens of thousands of people in the Plattsburgh/Burlington area and helped to spread the word about my undertaking and the Stand Up To Cancer cause. This exposure helped guide viewers to my Standing Cyclist website, where I had included links directly to the SU2C website. Here they could learn about the cause and easily donate funds directly to the organization. That was my mission and it was all working out even better than I had planned.

It didn't end there. Many others had learned about my attempt and purpose and were striking up conversations and cheering me on along the way. This included a Canadian reporter that had picked up the story and crossed the border into the U.S. to track my progress and film me on the move. This had all provided me with much needed positive energy, to help fuel my effort. I began to rely on this level of support as my condition worsened, particularly on that fifth day of standing cycling. I would have liked to read and learn about other techniques and tools, both mental and physical, for attempting such a bizarre challenge but as I had discovered, no one else had a history of touring, saddle-less, for a cause or any other reason. I had no one else to draw knowledge, inspiration or motivation from. No other standing cyclist, anyway. I needed that positive fuel from my local supporters and from all those impacted by all forms of Cancer, everywhere. The population I was standing up for.

Soon I rolled back out of town and into a more rural setting, for the final leg of my day's route. My mind captured thoughts of how bad I was feeling before my various cheerleaders arrived to follow my progress. It made me once again revisit egoic energy vs. feelings of true altruism. When others cheer us on to win a race or accomplish something great for charity, is this incoming energy just an ego feed or can it become something more. Something bigger. I knew I had to watch this carefully. I was out there for others, not myself, but when people are talking and writing about you and what you're doing, it becomes easy to lose focus. For a moment you think, "Wow, I must really be something!" That's when it all falls apart.

When you set out to raise awareness or funds for something special, you have to take on more of a supporting cast member role. Put simply, it's not the "me" show and you are not really the star. You have to redirect every compliment, every cheer and every kind thought, back outward, with a deep sense of gratitude of course. That redirection becomes very difficult to do when you push yourself to such an extreme that you end up requiring that energy, just to carry on. This was an epiphany for me. I began to consciously evaluate myself. My thoughts and actions, when in action. Early in life, we often do good things for self-serving reasons. For fuel. For recognition. Or perhaps to convey an essence of who we want to be and be seen as. Now, watching this tendency in my own self, I felt as if I was now finally growing up. I was learning to selflessly receive and redirect that incoming excitement and positive support, to the core of my purpose. The purpose of serving others, using this unique ability, passion and interest as a vehicle. Not for attention, not for image, but simply because I could and should.

"Crap!" Nothing like an angry Pit Bull on a thin little rope, to wake you up from waking up. I'm actually a Pit fan while off the bike, but there's something about bicycles that turn otherwise friendly pups into Cujo. I've even had cute little poodles foam at the mouth as I coasted passed on my two-wheeler. It seemed like the New York side of the lake was especially dangerous with regards to angry dogs. Dog dispositions definitely lightened up a bit on the Vermont side.

I rolled into the little town of Westport, NY just before dinner time. I planned to land at a local hotel and made my way across town to check in before dark, hoping to bag a good meal, a cold beer, a clean bed and a hot shower. As it turned out, I scored all of the above. The hotel was a quaint Inn with a friendly staff. The owner wasn't around the night I arrived, but his daughter Stephanie checked me in and guided me to where I could lock up my bicycle for the evening.

When bicycle touring, standing or sitting, "Leave No Trace" applies just as it does when hiking and backpacking. Well, that night I didn't exactly fulfill my responsibility. I was having some trouble walking, as well as thinking and speaking. Apparently, I failed to successfully navigate around the flower vase which sat atop an outside dinner table, after securing my bike around back. I don't remember bumping the table. In fact, at the time, I could have sworn I hadn't. After only the first 10 minutes of my stay at this tidy Inn, I wrecked the joint. Sheepishly, I presented Stephanie with a pile of wet flowers and several pieces of broken vase, along with my apologies. Quick-witted, she immediately grinned, bowed and said, "For me?" Suddenly I didn't feel like such a klutz and was able to laugh it off, as we combed the outside decking on our hands and knees for any remaining sharp splinters of porcelain.

After a quick nap and a hot shower, I headed downstairs for a large dinner, dessert and a glass of red wine. Just what I needed at this point in the trip. I replayed that day's 45 miles of standing cycling, in my mind. Part of me couldn't believe I had completed another big day riding this way. I wanted to be proud of myself but this challenge is far from over, I thought. I sat quietly alone for over an hour and stared across the small but well-organized dining room at other diners and wondered what they did that day. Did they go sightseeing? Maybe they drove around in their comfy Euro sedans and went shopping at nearby strip malls. I wanted to go up to them and ask about their world, and tell them my own story, but I couldn't figure out exactly how to open the conversation. I had learned on several occasions already just how tricky it is to explain what I was doing, even when people would actually see me in action. You have to remember, Stand Up To Cancer was still a relatively new organization. Not many in that area had heard of it, which is exactly why I was out there. At times, I would introduce myself and when asked what I was doing, I would smile and say I'm bicycle touring around Lake Champlain, without a seat, for Stand Up To Cancer. Some would look at me like I had two heads and others would think I was kidding around and half-laugh, politely, just in case I was in fact, serious. Then there was the too often asked question, "No seat...do you just sit on a post?" Then it was my turn to laugh.

After a great night's sleep, I was ready for day 6 and my second Adirondack region leg of this tour which would take me from Westport down to Whitehall, NY. Day 6 would prove to be the longest and most difficult day, in terms of overall effort, out of all 8. Based on the previous day, my maps and my knowledge of this region, I knew I'd want and need a hotel by sundown. I would come to discover later that Whitehall is a hot spot for Bigfoot sightings, so in hindsight, I was bummed that I hadn't camped out that night. Now that would have been something really worth journaling about.

That day would also prove to be my most social. I had the opportunity to connect with soccer moms running a charity bake sale, corner store owners, a Whitehall Police Officer, road runners and fellow cyclists. Each time, I was able to share my mission and surprisingly, they got it. We talked Cancer. Strangers began sharing their own stories with me, sometimes along the shoulder of a lonely country road. Their struggles, acceptance, and triumphs. It was a chilly day but I was warmed by the kindness and support of those special people and their inspiring memories. We spoke about Patrick Swayze, who had passed just days before, as previously mentioned. I left behind piles of Standing Cyclist business cards, which I had printed before I left Pennsylvania. These cards would help direct people to my website, where they could learn more about SU2C, track my progress around the Lake via the SPOT Satellite Messenger I was carrying on my handlebar pack, and donate directly to the organization. I began to realize I was sitting (or standing I should say) at the hub of something very cool, and it was my privilege. Part of me felt guilty. Guilty for enjoying my adventure, when the community I was riding for was enduring such suffering. After all, I was simply doing what I love. What comes naturally to me. I ride bikes, I always have. I thought a lot about that guilt, that day, while riding alone on heavily wooded roads, nestled between the western shore of Lake Champlain and the East Shore of Lake George, NY.

My Allergic Asthma was now becoming a compelling, secondary point of interest while circumnavigating Lake Champ. I met adult Asthmatics who were very curious about my story. However, it was the parents of Asthmatic children that were most confused and blown away by the attempt, with or without medication. Unfortunately, I could tell that some of these people viewed their children as hopelessly sickly. I suspect after many gut wrenching midnight emergency room visits, emotionally drained family members begin to lean toward limited thinking and overprotective parenting, and away from positive thinking, and the belief that anything is possible. My heart went out to them and I wanted to help.

These connections provided me with numerous opportunities to explain my own personal Asthma Management philosophy. I usually begin with, "Mindful living!" I break it down into stress management, diet, fitness, rest/recovery and environmental (or trigger avoidance). I would explain that contrary to popular belief, Asthma can be positively impacted by self-awareness, deep reflection, meditation and mindful decision making. For example, in my case, eating fast processed foods along with other factors such as lack of sleep, and generally mindless behavior caused problems for me. I began to improve, almost immediately, when I started to reflect on my own decisions, their effects and make positive changes. In every instance, my information and energy were well received.

Cycling can be a perfect metaphor for life. First and foremost, it's about balance. No matter how robust your legs and mind are, without balance you're on the ground and going nowhere. When our lives fall out of balance, we shift off center. We lean over and lose control of our own well-being. Disease may see an opening and takes full advantage of the opportunity. In terms of medication, there are of course serious ailments that may require medication, much like clinical depression and forms of severe anxiety, however, it has been my own experience that Asthma is often overmedicated and at times can be very well managed through education, balanced living and mindfulness practice.

Many medications simply alleviate pain and discomfort, temporarily, without addressing the root cause of the problem. The actual cause of an attack. In the case of Allergic Asthma, medication may prevent or lessen the effects of a serious Asthma incident, however, I do not believe medication alone is the one and only long-term solution. Other factors must be considered and addressed. Patients must be viewed and treated as a whole person. If it wasn't for the open-minded, big picture, long-term view of my own healthcare providers and holistic healers I would have never gotten on a bicycle again. I may not even have gotten on with life itself.

Halfway to Whitehall, I was slowing down considerably. I was 30 miles into a 60-mile day and I was fading fast. After resisting thoughts of stopping for the night and camping near the historic town of Ticonderoga, at the northern-most tip of Lake George and significantly shy of my day's goal, I rolled on through Putnam Center and Dresden. Having now fully committed, in my own mind, to Whitehall as my evening destination, I called ahead to secure a simple room somewhere in town. Now I just needed to get there. Oddly enough, aggressive dogs that bummed me out earlier in my trip now served as much needed shots of adrenaline. Three shots to be exact. Three big, growling shots.

The weather was working against me as well. The chilly but dry air was cracking my swollen lower lip to the point of steady bleeding. I was also nauseous from my various concoctions of athletic supplements which included additional, unfamiliar products picked up along the way. As I rode standing, my stomach would rise and fall with each pedal stroke, shifting its contents in a disconcerting way. I swore I would vomit at any moment. Hopefully, not on a cheering bystander or local news reporter. I glanced down at my heart rate monitor and realized I had been riding for over 8 hours. It had also calculated my caloric output at over 4,000 kcal. Knowing my caloric intake was significantly less up to that point in the day, I realized I needed fuel and I needed it soon. At that point, anything would do. I pulled off and grabbed a fatty ham sandwich and a full bottle of sports drink at the nearest corner store. Convenience store pork never tasted so good.

Whitehall was now coming into view. I had several miles to travel along a quiet main road before dropping into town to search out my home base for the evening. By the time I rolled down through the narrow, busy streets of this Sasquatchy little town, I was toast. I felt like my bike was riding me, and not the other way around. My brain and legs were shutting down. Oddly enough, just about every system in my body was rebelling with the notable exception of my lungs. I was breathing stronger than ever. I couldn't believe it. The one thing I thought would give out first, turned out to be my greatest strength of the day. As I wobbled through red traffic lights and stop signs, I was lucky I didn't get run over. Just then Officer Dan came into view. Usually, when I see a police officer while out cycling or driving a car, I get those weird, guilty butterflies in my stomach as many of us do. Whether I was doing something wrong, or not. Not this time. I was careless and clueless. I practically rolled into his police cruiser. Turns out, luckily, Officer Dan was an athlete himself and we swapped stories for a bit before he escorted me down through town to my motel, no brain power on my part required. I was grateful for the guidance and protection, while muscling through my stupor.

Priscilla and her family were expecting me. After standing and riding for almost 11 hours, I came to a stop around 6pm that night, on the front stoop of a small Budget Inn. Even though my mind and body were fried, I was able to muster a friendly smile and an abbreviated explanation of what I was doing out on the road. Quickly, what seemed like all of Priscilla's family appeared from behind the check-in counter. Soon, we were all discussing Cancer and the toll it had taken on friends and family. They were impressed with my effort and made me as comfortable as I could be, given the circumstances. Once again, I experienced that familiar pang of guilt. Here I am swimming in the positive attention, feeling like I'm fluffing my own feathers. I silently kicked in a humbling little mantra I had created and repeated earlier that day, as I turned and hobbled away to find my room. "You may be doing IT, but IT'S not about you." The positive support and energy was priceless, and much needed, but I could never become attached to it. It always needed to be redirected to its proper home. Toward the hearts of those for whom I was riding.

After a lame shuffle across the street for a chicken parm hero and some garlic bread, I headed back to the Inn to gear up for the following day's leg. I sat out front awhile and looked up at the stars, nursing my full bursting belly, stiff legs and floppy ankles. I took some time to quietly consider how far I had come. Honestly, I couldn't believe I was still rolling. A part of me had doubted that I would ever get that far without sitting down. Another part of me actually fantasized about breaking a pedal or crankarm. The perfect excuse to end this madness and go home, with head held high. Of course, that was never really an option. I knew deep down that I owed it to those I rode for, to finish what I had begun

300 miles ago. I was going to roll back into Burlington. It just had to be that way.

That night proved to be a challenge almost equal to my previous day out on the route. First it was the pain. My legs, arms and wrists locked up and cramped with such ferocity that I had to get up and move around and stretch several times an hour, throughout much of the night. I had purchased lip balm the evening before, but now I reconsidered applying it to my bloody, burning lower lip. In my fatigued logic, I strategically decided that my lip pain may help distract me from the pain screaming out from other parts of my body, so I could get at least some much needed rest. As it turned out, it worked...for a while. Then came the Asthma. The delayed effects of my hard, lengthy riding day caught up with me around 3am. Bad news. This, combined with the often stuffy room conditions experienced when hotel touring, made rest and rejuvenation impossible. I would have to ride my next 50-mile leg on little-to-no sleep.

Day 7 began way too early, and way too slowly. My pace was so far off I knew I would be lucky to finish the day at my target campground in Chimney Point, VT, before sundown. Setting up camp, checking over the bike, eating and completing various other camp and personal chores after dark, after riding all day, is never preferred. Every little task is 10 times more difficult under those challenging conditions. I would do it if I had to, as I had done many times before, but my worn self would much appreciate the alternative.

My usually fair sense of direction was apparently impaired by my sleepless night back at the Inn, and I got lost twice while rolling out of town. Four gun shots, three dogs, one bee sting and one hour later, I made it out. Not far outside of Whitehall, I ran into two other touring cyclists and we swapped stories while riding along the shoulder of Bay Rd. I appreciated the brief taste of camaraderie.

My 7th day along this route was surely my worst Asthma day. It had all the makings. A difficult prior day, a bad night's sleep, intense heat, maximum exertion, lack of healthy whole foods, loose hills, and long stretches of dusty dirt roads. I kept replaying my little balanced living Asthma speech in my own head to get by, then eventually thinking to myself, "Hey dummy, you're doing exactly the opposite of what you preach! No wonder why you have an elephant sitting on your chest! Pull over butthead! Things are way out of balance." I pulled over. I thought about walking my loaded rig for a few miles, for a much needed rest, however it's far more awkward and energy zapping to push than you would expect. It's configured well for riding but not for carrying or pushing. I pulled out a bandana to wrap around my mouth and nose, to keep some of the dust out of my insides.

At this point, I was struggling to breathe even while standing still, forget about standing cycling. Here began the most frightening point of my entire Lake Champ Stand Up To Cancer challenge. I was in the middle of nowhere. I think I was drooling. I ran out of juice, couldn't breathe and knew that if

I used my rescue inhaler I would further raise my already near maximum heart rate. Pinning my heart rate would be a risky thing under these circumstances, but not using my rescue inhaler may result in a full-on Asthma attack. I didn't know what to do. My normal human reaction was of course to panic. I knew I had only one viable option at that moment. Meditation. I moved myself to the shade and stood motionless. I've been here before, I thought. No worries. Stay present. Watch the panic. Simply recognize it. Watch your breath. Breathe in, breathe out. Focus on your heart rate. Bump bump. Bump bump. The whole time I did this I had my inhaler close by. I have an unshakeable faith in the divine tapestry of all things and that I am (we are) never really alone, but I knew I needed to do my part. I needed to guide myself through the storm. Just be. Stay present. Let go. All is fine. Breathe in, breathe out. Stay focused. Don't make this worse than it needs to be. Rock solid. Rock solid. Finally, I was able to semi-confidently place my inhaler back into my handlebar bag. I wasn't 100% but I was functional, and I needed to get back to work. I carefully rolled off to continue my adventure.

Many endurance athletes speak about bursting emotions when undertaking something extreme. Something seemingly epic. I had never considered myself an endurance athlete but I would soon understand this phenomenon as it applied to my quest to complete this ride standing up. When you commit fully to such an undertaking and give all you have to give, there's a point where you stall. Even if it's just for a moment or two. It's more than muscle fatigue, low blood sugar or mal-functioning brain parts. In its very worst case, it feels like a depletion or clog of cellular and spiritual energy. Energy some refer to as Chi or Prana. Whether or not this life force originates from the inside or outside of the body, or perhaps both, is still a great mystery to most. When we are granted with a resurgence of this energy throughout our system, an emotional volcano may erupt from within and our heart cracks open. We break and are then repaired or, at the very least, become repairable. This is more than positive thinking, ego or any of the like. I know this for certain, deep down in-side, as I have experienced this many times since while standing cycling in extreme circumstances.

Perhaps my most significant heart crack occurred between Whitehall and Chimney Point, on day 7. After recovering somewhat from my breathing incident miles back, I used up what seemed to be nearly all my remaining physical, emo-tional and spiritual energy. I no longer believed I could finish this epic multiday ride. I was no longer confident I would re-turn home safely. Worst of all, I was now almost completely disconnected from Stand Up To Cancer and their noble cause. In my mind, what was left of it, I just didn't care any-more. Part of me was angry that I was in this position at all. I thought, "Who really cares about what I'm doing out here, anyway?" I pulled off at a corner store. Why, I can't recall. I was no longer thirsty or hungry. I was beyond both. I was out-of-body, pissed off and just plain done. I floated through the store on autopilot, bought a ready-made sandwich and a pretty purple sports drink simply because it caught my blood-shot eye. I think I tossed out some Standing Cyclist cards in my stupor. Who knows.

I wandered outside and sat on the stoop out front of the little general store and started lazily consuming my pro-cessed food and colored water. As an energetic being, I was tangled up and stuck at the bottom of all bottoms. Suddenly, I was surprised by a woman who seemingly appeared out of nowhere, although I later guessed she had exited from a car in the parking lot around back. Time was speeding up and slowing down, at weird intervals. I was trying to stay focused and present, but I was weak, dizzy and physically vibrating. As the woman approached me, my mind instantly and nega-tively thought, "Oh no, I'm going to have to talk aren't I?" I sat silently as she came close, leaned over, looked me square in the eyes and smiled wide. She said in a firm yet fragile voice, "I know who you are. You have no idea how much what you're doing out here means to us." She touched my arm gently, still smiling, then slowly walked off. To this day, I can't recall if she went into the store or back to her car. Then it happened. My heart cracked wide open and my guts fell out onto the pavement. At least that's what it felt like. As I sat sobbing quietly, a rejuvenating energy entered my center-most point. I found myself awake and crystal clear in my mission, much like in the weeks and months following my fa-ther's passing when I was forced to engage life, for the first time, as a mature adult. My breathing was comfortable and my body was loose and ready. I finished my sandwich and drank some clear water before rolling back out onto the route. Something had just happened. Something unusual. Something important. It stayed with me for the remainder of that difficult day, through the completion of my trip, and into the rest of my life. Into the second half of my life. It was now clear I would make it up to Chimney Point, and beyond. But no one said it would be pretty.

The physical and emotional ups and downs continued for several more hours, but that special charge I received kept me rolling forward and into Chimney Point campground around 7pm that evening. I closed out the day at 51 standing miles. The office was closed for the night so I claimed a small tent space at the back of the property near a creek which thinking back was more like a swamp. As I settled in for the night I couldn't help think about the classic thriller, The Creature from the Black Lagoon. In my groggy state, I could hear strange swamp sounds through my thin tent wall. It wasn't raining that night but I opted to use my trusty pee bag rather than brave the imaginary creature that lurked beyond my now extinguished campfire.

I woke fairly fresh and positive the next morning only to find a cruddy water bottle and camp garbage spread out around my tent. I was so utterly exhausted the night before that I, once again, failed to clean the endurance powder residue from my main water bottle. I boiled some water and built a makeshift bottle brush from broken branches to clean up and sterilize the inside surface. While the water boiled, I cleaned up the debris neighboring critters must have nibbled through during the night. Turns out, judging by the tracks I had found, the only big, scary swamp monster at Chimney Point was an adolescent raccoon.

As I rode off on my last day out-of-the-saddle, I couldn't help think of that woman from the day before. I couldn't get her supportive energy and warmth out of my mind. Was this a sign, I questioned? A guardian angel looking out for me? The kindness of others and odd coincidences continued. In the middle of that last day, day 8, I stopped for a moment on the shoulder of the road not far from Burlington, Vermont, my final destination. As I chomped down my energy bar, I spotted a cyclist slowly rolling up on me from the south. As she got closer I noticed she was an older woman riding a modern road bike. She had no panniers and saddlebags so I knew she had to be a local. She stopped and we chatted for about 15 minutes. She was a life-long cyclist, Vermont resident, and just recently celebrated her 70th birthday. This athletic elder was in excellent shape, sporting long lean limbs and a slim waistline. She asked me about my tour and I was happy to chat up Stand Up To Cancer, my purpose, and my progress. She had a gentle yet strong way about her. I could tell from the way she spoke that she had a complex, emotional history. Perhaps she's a survivor, I thought. Maybe she had lost a loved one to Cancer or some other disease. Intuitively, I knew not to ask.

We talked about camping and biking and how beautiful my trip had turned out to be, with lake views and forests well beyond my original expectations. We both shared a love for the natural world and compared memories of our own wilderness adventures, along the road side, until we both knew it was time to part ways. Neither one of us wanted it to end, but we both had work to do. I felt like I knew her my entire life. Maybe through many lifetimes. When we began to shift our pedals in preparation to roll away, she took my hand in hers, smiled lovingly and with great intensity said, "My name is Mary and it's been a pleasure meeting you. Good luck on the rest of your journey." As she rolled away, I thought of Mother Mary from my Roman Catholic childhood, and another very special Mary. A strong woman who, only a couple years earlier, had passed away from Breast Cancer. I had never met Mary but I had heard many wonderful stories about her kindness, courage and overall good character from those close to her, who are also close to me. Before I left home she was on my mind a great deal and throughout my trip as well. I now had a fresh reminder to carry me my remaining 28 miles into the city of Burlington, where I had begun my journey 8 long days earlier. Thank you Mary. All three of you.

The last leg of my adventure had me rolling down beautifully paved paths, alongside Lake Champlain, finally crossing into the city of Burlington. This was it, I thought. I was almost done. I leaned back on my pedals, hunched forward, and stretched my back out as I flew around sharp turns and passed local marinas. Everything was perfect. The temperature was ideal, the breeze invigorating, the scenery magical and the energy of the moment perfectly balanced.

I rolled into the parking lot of the motel where I had left my car. I had called ahead. They knew I'd be staying the night. After hauling everything sloppily into my ground floor room, I fell back onto my bed, stared up at the ceiling and cried. I'd like to describe what I was feeling but honestly, I don't think I was thinking at all. I just...was. I did have a keen sense of my body and what hurt. I massaged my legs and arms for I don't really know how long. Time was useless. I would realize and record later that I had completed my final day of riding, standing up, in just shy of 8 hours and logged 53.2 miles. Beer. Steak. Sleep. In what order? In that order, I thought.

I managed to hobble down the street, in the dark, for a late night solo celebration. As I sat in the center of town, at the same outside eatery that helped launch my trip one week before, I observed the tourists and locals meander past my table as I inhaled a long awaited Guinness. As before, I tried to read their faces and body language. I wondered if they were working through a serious illness or loved someone who was. I wondered if they were grieving. I wanted to grab them, hold them and tell them everything would be okay, but I knew that wasn't necessarily true. Sometimes things simply don't work out the way we want them to, and we are forced to accept and work with that, in the best way that we can. Forced to find balance between the pleasant and unpleasant.

I thought about my previous cycling adventures, my Allergic Asthma, lost loved ones, and all of the suffering and kindness which graced my Lake Champlain route. All of the ups and all of the downs. As I sat there with throbbing legs and cramping fingers, my eyes caught a giggling little girl running across the courtyard and everything was clear. Yes, it's true that life sometimes disappoints us, pains us, even destroys us, but none of that makes a well-lived life any less perfect. As for those of us seeking to make a difference, it is in the doing itself that helps change the world. As it has always been, I suspect, since the beginning of time.

Chapter 8 - THE MESO CHALLENGE

Fast forward. Larry Davis didn't strike me as a hugger, so you can imagine his surprise when I bear hugged him good-bye as we stood on the sidewalk in Washington D.C., at the close of our 2010 Meso Challenge Standing Cyclist Event. I hadn't known Larry very long and most of our communication had been through email, texting and a couple of cell phone calls while on the go. That moment in D.C. would be my last significant connection with Larry before his passing from Mesothelioma Cancer.

Rewind. When Larry's daughter, Courtney Davis, and I first spoke about this solo standing cycling event many months before, we couldn't have envisioned its outcome. Much like my previous adventures, this had never been done. Not exactly in this manner, anyway. I was sure it could be done. I just didn't know if I could actually do it. To clarify, I would be riding the off-road Allegheny and C&O Towpaths, standing up the entire way from Pittsburgh, PA to Washington, D.C.

By this time, multi-day standing tours were not unusual for me, but this trip would raise the bar quite high. I would be relatively self-contained, camping out every night, unsupported and I would be riding a custom fixed-gear single-speed standing cycle. This would mean no gears, no seat and...no coasting...ever. Fixed gear bikes are direct drive which means when the bicycle is rolling, your legs are moving and vice versa. Unless you stop for a drink or bathroom break, there's no rest. Much like running, the downhills can be just as tough as the uphills. You have to carefully pace yourself at all times to avoid fatigue and bonking. For an Allergic Asthma sufferer, this pacing would prove to be especially tricky.

In the past, as previously mentioned, I would avoid Asthma incidents in large part, by monitoring and minimizing my heart rate on long rides standing up. On my previous standing tours, I was able to throttle back my heart rate by coasting the flats and downhills when needed. For this trip, and all training leading up to the start date, coasting was not an option. Also not an option was failure. I made that decision early on and that notion remained in my head the entire time.

I would be riding for several important reasons, all of which meant a great deal to me. First and foremost, it was to honor Larry and his extensive efforts to educate the public on the dangers of Asbestos, the material that causes Mesothelioma. This material has a long history of being used irresponsibly by profit-hungry companies throughout the 20th Century. A combination of poor employee education and lack of adequate safety regulations, exposed hundreds of thousands of laborers and craftsmen, and their loved ones, to this Cancer-causing fiber. Thousands of people are suffering and dying each year because of greed and negligence, changing their own and their families' lives forever. I saw this firsthand during my time with Larry, and through Courtney's suffering as a family member as well.

Larry's story touched me in a way that none other had, to that point in my life. Of course, we all know someone who has been challenged by some type of Cancer. It was that common thread that fueled my Stand Up To Cancer tour, but this was different. Here you have a man-made, definitive cause. Asbestos was first classified as a carcinogen back in the early 1900's. It was mind-blowing to me that many countries in the world, including the United States, had not fully banned the use of Asbestos. I began to feel the helplessness, frustration and grief of the Meso community. I could not sit still. I could not sit at all. I needed to stand up for them, in the only way I knew how. I would ride. Ride to raise awareness and funds for the Mesothelioma Applied Research Foundation, in honor of Larry and his ongoing activism to educate others and ban the use of Asbestos. Larry and Courtney had established "Action Against Asbestos," a robust website dedicated to the cause. As I toured the 330+ miles from PA to D.C., I would stop along the way to discuss the cause and direct people to their website to learn more and donate funds to the foundation, via Larry's donation page.

The delicate balance each day would include riding time, "cause" chores, camp chores and physical/mental recovery. I knew I'd have to average about 50 miles per day, while still packing in everything else. During the planning stage, months before, it just wasn't adding up. There wouldn't be enough time in the day. Knowing how I tend to overextend myself, what would likely suffer would be my recovery time and that wouldn't fly. After a couple of days, I might still be rolling but I wouldn't be able to articulate well enough to serve the cause along the way. This wasn't just an unusually challenging endurance event, it was a tribute and a fundraiser. If I couldn't strategize and speak well, I might succeed physically but I would blow the bigger picture. I kept this in mind as I built my new standing fixed-gear bike and began my highly specialized training.

For the bike, I settled on a bright green Felt Curbside urban fixed-gear model. Original equipment included skinny road tires, a delicate radially spoked front wheel and some oddly colorful frame pads. It would prove to be a solid base to work from, and that frame remains part of my primary standing bicycle at the time of this writing. The first thing I did was strip it down and start sketching out my modifications. Of course, I began by removing the seat and seatpost. I removed the seat-tube clamp from the frame and cut the top off the seat-tube to reduce the standover height and prevent the re-installation of a seat down the road. I fill most of my empty seat-tubes with steel wool and expanding foam, then cap it. Once rigid, the foamy steel concoction makes the installation of a post/seat impossible. I do this to quiet the naysayers who believe I keep a spare seat and post in my pannier bags for when I get tired. Next, I raised my cockpit by adding my now typical high-rise BMX bars and a BMX stem, mounted to new rigid steel forks with rack braze-ons and an uncut steerer tube to position my back at just the right angle for this fixed-gear configuration. Not too far forward, as in previous designs, but still not quite vertical. I swapped out the front wheel for something beefier and bought some new, slightly wider tires well-suited for hardpack dirt paths. I installed front and rear racks to the frame and had test fit my pannier bags to both. As always, I went with simple, open downhill mountain bike pedals. They allow me to easily shift foot positions on the fly but most importantly they can take a beating. Constant pedaling while standing, especially off-road, results in excessive downward forces. Strong components are a must.

As Courtney, Larry and I continued to work through the technical details of the trip remotely via email/telephone, my full-scale body/mind training in Pennsylvania was in full spin. Lack of trip time remained my number one problem and still needed to be addressed. I needed to figure out a way to crush 50+ miles a day standing up without coasting, and still have time to stop and speak intelligently. After experimenting with various body positions, pacing, gear ratios and average heart rates, I was still smoked even at half my target mileage. It was clear that a near double, rolling marathon on this type of bike would leave me with little to no gas in my tank to fuel anything else. That's when it hit me. I had been thinking like a cyclist. I needed to think and train more like a runner, but from a cyclist's perspective. It was around that time that I began referring to my standing fixed-gear cycling style, as "Rolling", a perceived cross between cycling and running. Somewhere in this mindshift, I found my answer. If I could relax more and cycle "in-flow" mechanically one-with-the-bike, whether ascending or descending, I could expend less energy which would keep me sharper throughout each riding day and reduce my recovery time and effort between days.

The theory felt right, so I began to experiment with that approach. At first, it wasn't working. In fact, I felt more fatigued than before. It took several weeks of varying cadence (full pedal rotations per minutes), the angle of my back, the position of my feet atop the pedals, tire pressure and hand positions, before I made any real progress. Finally, I had the perfect body/bike combination to maximize my output without short circuiting my physiology. "Rolling" as it turned out, was a new style of riding that required a new style of training. Later I would integrate breath/pedal stroke alignment and mindfulness meditation-in-motion into my Rolling, which would change everything for me, yet again. It would allow me, an otherwise ordinary individual, to accomplish extraordinary things on that particular bike.

Both the beginning and end point of this trip were not accidental. Pittsburgh was meant to represent industrial America. A typical factory town with a strong potential of Asbestos-related diseases. It was also noteworthy in that Larry himself spent time as a young person in that area. A time during which construction demolition was common place, launching Asbestos into the air, within the surrounding areas. Washington D.C. symbolized both the end of the line and drawing of the line. A political point in space and time that represented change. A place where Asbestos could be banned once and for all, within the United States. Both Larry and the Mesothelioma Applied Research Foundation were already heavily engaged in that D.C. mission.

As it turned out, two adjacent towpaths, with a deep history, ran from one region to the next. In the north, The Great Allegheny Passage starts just outside of Pittsburgh, PA and extends 135 miles southeast to Cumberland, MD. At Cumberland, it joins the Chesapeake & Ohio (C&O) Canal Towpath which runs an additional 185 miles into D.C. The total route from Pittsburgh to D.C. would take me 7 days to complete. I would be Rolling through long, dark tunnels and I would bed down not far from famous Civil War battlefields. The trail surface is mostly crushed limestone and hardpack dirt, with only slight up and down grades along the way. For most, the trail conditions are perfect. For me, on this trip, I had to consider airborne trail dust on dry days and soggy energy-zapping mud when it rained. But overall, it was a terrific route for this particular attempt.

After months of planning and training, I was ready to Roll. On August 23, 2010, I packed my car and drove out to western PA. For logistical reasons, I had decided to begin my trip near McKeesport, a Pittsburgh suburb. My base would be the

Yough Shore Inn, where the fresh new friendship and hospitality of Dolores, Tom and Lin would seed my journey with great fun and joy. I would leave my car at the back of the Inn where it would remain safe until my return one week later. I could pick up the Allegheny trail right down the road from their Inn. No complex shuttling required. The food, convenient location and camaraderie were the perfect combination and the best way to kick off such a trip.

Day 1 led me from my starting point near McKeesport to a little camping area near Adelaide, PA. Early into the ride, I hooked up with Pat Cloonan for a local newspaper interview and photoshoot at a nearby Cafe. I also connected with Joyce and Bob MacGregor who maintain a newsletter about the trail and local happenings. The Cafe was known for Allegheny trail riders coming through for good food and like-minded company. The best part was, they allowed cyclists to write on their walls with a magic marker. How cool is that? I dated my attempt and signed "Standing Cyclist" to reinforce my intentions. We shared some chow and a couple of laughs, before I headed on down the trail. Both the local newspaper article and the MacGregors' support helped raise awareness and funds for the Meso/Ban Asbestos cause early on in the week. The rendezvous cost me 5 miles of backtracking but this kickstart made it well worth it.

After a few small mechanical issues, several unscented (Allergic Asthma-friendly) sunscreen applications, and about 3 hours of moderate riding, I pulled off-trail for a quick food break in West Newton. I locked my bike up for a few minutes to hit a restroom and came back to find a lady puffing away on her cigarette, right over the top of my panniers. "Really?" I thought. Just as I was about to say something she turned around to walk off and inadvertently blew smoke right at me, as I approached. It took me a few moments to pull it together and by then she was gone. I was steamed. With all the space out here, I thought, she had to smoke Cancer sticks in my space and blow smoke in my face. I wondered if her knowing about my breathing challenges and the purpose of my trip would have impacted her mindless actions and lackadaisical attitude.

Water and electrolytes are, of course, critical for life and especially important when cycling or running long distances. Early on in that trip it was clear that high daytime temperatures, combined with infrequent water sources, would become a serious consideration. Even on day 1, what I thought would be a water stop came up dry. Rockbottom was a primitive pit stop listed on route maps as a viable water source but when I arrived I found no potable water. I decided to continue on to Adelaide. As I had done on previous trips, I was carrying extra water and electrolyte powder, but on that first day, I had run out of H2O. I had successfully paced my output but failed to pace my hydration. Due to the rising humidity and my new no-coasting riding style, my sweat rate exceeded what I had expected. Sweat rate is particularly key in any endurance event. It's fairly simple to consider. If you sweat out more water than you take in, you will likely become dehydrated sooner than later. Dehydration often occurs before you even recognize it's happening. Cramps, confusion, and extreme fatigue are soon experienced and eventually, if not corrected, the situation can become life threatening. As the saying goes, if you're thirsty you're already shifting toward some level of dehydration. On hot days, during any intense athletic activity, you need to take in a small amount of water with electrolytes, at fairly regular intervals whether or not you feel the need. This keeps you healthy, well-tuned for performance, and increases your overall chances of success in your endeavor.

I wearily rode into camp around 5:30pm that night and immediately sought out a water source, chugging down at least one liter's worth. Throughout the day, I had stuck to my well-paced, "conservation of energy" game plan and was now feeling very good about my stamina and brain power. I rode my fixed-gear standing cycle for over 6.5 hours in total (actual pedaling time) and fell just shy of 50 miles that first day. My 116 BPM average heart rate was perfect for this new Rolling style of riding and all was good. I had good weather, met great people, spread good information about the cause, raised money, logged respectable miles and still had time and energy left in reserve.

I had the great pleasure of connecting with Bryce and Bill, two very cool former BMX bicycle racers, who were passing through camp while touring the Great Allegheny Passage.

They loved what I was attempting and were fascinated by my bike design and riding style. I was a bit envious of their camaraderie. Touring alone, when all is well, is an amazing experience but when times get tough, as in life, a good riding partner can be the difference between success and failure.

I soon noticed another solo bikepacker not far down the hill from my own tent. As I watched him complete several camp chores, I noticed some odd behaviors. In my weakened state, my mind shifted too easily from observation to evaluation to judgment, and I quickly labeled him introverted, quirky and disturbed. Maybe even dangerous. Soon my mind wandered to silly "What If?" scenarios, like "What if he comes into my camp tonight and attacks me in my sleep?" Yep, I had this guy pegged. He was bad news and I remained on high alert.

Later on, I sat back near my tent, gazed up at the stars and reflected on the day. I conducted the normal assessment of my progress and my current condition. Quads hurt. Ankles sore. Nothing too serious to report. Breathing? Yes, still breathing and I can still feel my toes. Always a good thing. It appeared that my in-flow Rolling meditation approach to riding this bizarre bike was working. At least on day 1. Time would tell if my new methods and training efforts would pay off for the remainder of the trip.

Before rolling up inside my light sleeping sack, I called home to check in and called Larry to update him on my progress. I was utilizing my satellite tracking device, as I had done while riding around Lake Champlain and Iceland, so I knew Larry and Courtney could see my position real-time but I also knew a call would be important. I felt like Larry and I were riding this trip together, but of course given his current condition, it was in spirit only. Larry's Mesothelioma was quite advanced. He had been diagnosed several years earlier and the prognosis was not good. Few Mesothelioma patients survive past several years. Larry would thrive over 4 years. Larry was also a lifelong runner who had organized and served as Race Director for the South Florida Miles for Meso annual running event. By the middle of 2013, Larry had directly and posthumously raised over $100,000 for the Applied Mesothelioma Research Foundation and donations made in his name continue to roll in.

Reflecting back on Larry's accomplishments, however, I believe his greatest impact on the Meso community was his attitude. He didn't view himself as a poor, unfortunate victim that required our pity. This allowed other Meso sufferers and their families to embody that same strength while living with and working through their own health challenges. Sometimes hope, courage and the energy to change what is wrong, holds equal, perhaps greater value, than money. Yes, I believe Larry needed to hear my voice but not half as much as I needed to hear his. His encouragement that evening helped put me to sleep while still revving me up for the many days ahead.

I woke on day 2 feeling a little weaker than usual. I did a short walking meditation and also reflected on my performance so far. I thought about my metabolism. I didn't feel like I consumed enough food the day before. My heart rate monitor log confirmed this, showing I had burned over 4,500 kcal throughout Day 1 compared to my relatively low 2700 kcal intake. With an average heart rate well within my weight management zone, I was clearly operating at a deficit. At home, on a training day, this wouldn't be a bad thing but out there tripping long-term, this was not so good. I needed more fuel for my engine. Good fuel, not junk food. I made some dietary adjustments that morning that would prove to be invaluable later on in my journey.

As I wrapped up camp, I recalled a dream I had the night before. The weird guy next door was in the starring role. He had come into my camp to offer me something. I couldn't see exactly what it was in my dream but I felt I couldn't accept it and turned him away abruptly because I viewed him, even in my dream state, as strange and dangerous.

Oddly enough, in my waking state, just as I was ready to Roll out to begin my day he walked up the hill toward my now barren campsite, stopped at my bike, and glanced over at me shyly. He had something in his hand. Still a bit groggy, I waited for him to speak first. He looked down at the ground, grinned subtlety and held up a thick, well-worn book. He said it was his guidebook for this area and that he was almost done with his trip. He didn't need it anymore and wanted to give it to me. I suspect, he could tell that I was just starting out and might find it useful. Suddenly that weird guy down the hill just became quite human. Quite kind and gentle.

I thanked him sincerely for his offer but I chose not to accept his gift. I explained that I was traveling fast and light, and already had all the maps and info I needed. He cracked a knowing smile, unconvincingly said he understood and then, after shaking hands, we went our separate ways. I never did get his name and our conversation was brief, but our meeting had a lasting impact on me. I often replayed our chat in my mind, sometimes reversing roles. Trail lessons come in all shapes and sizes. To this day, I believe "the weird guy" was my trip teaching for kindness, and non-judgment.

I had put about 10 miles behind me when my dream popped back into mind. The dream in which my not so weird neighbor offered me something I was unable to accept. A guidebook for the trail or perhaps for life? I suppose I wasn't quite ready for either. He was right. I was just starting out, and in many ways, I could have used that book.

Later that morning I Rolled up on Phil and Lawana near Connellsville, PA. They were part of a large group of trail riders. We chatted a bit about the Meso cause and my trip. They couldn't believe what I was attempting and gave me more kudos than any one person deserves. Soon I had the entire team cheering me on and it felt great but as I Rolled off basking in my brief, virtual pat on the back, I swerved around a large Black Snake crossing the trail. A near miss that really got my heart pumping, reminiscent of my Black Snake race collision earlier in life. Yet another reptile themed wake up call. A reminder, I thought, to remain focused on the cause and Larry's challenges, rather than my own personal goals and accomplishments. After splitting from the other riders, I continued down the trail with my new mantra for the day fresh in my head – (still) not about me, (still) not about me.

Near trail mile marker 78, I stopped to catch my breath and review my map. Before I knew it, out of nowhere there was a huge yellow and black butterfly popping its wings right in front of my face. It was brilliant and continued to circle my head and my bike for at least 20 minutes. I had never experienced anything quite like that before. Any feelings of loneliness and fear I may have had, at that point, soon disappeared. I was feeling very connected to the natural world and I continued on reenergized.

Mountain Bikers will know it's not uncommon to collect small rocks and dirt inside your shoes while riding off-road but, on day 2, I must have removed a dozen sharp little stones before lunchtime. It was maddening at times. At one point, I was so tired, I considered leaving the thumbtacksized rock in my left shoe. I needed something to keep me distracted and on-point. This reminded me of my cracked lip pain and the welcomed distraction it provided during my Lake Champ trip.

When you get tired riding standing up, injuries happen. Just then as these thoughts ran through my mind, it happened. Due to poor form, from fatigue, my left foot slipped off the pedal. In an attempt to regain control over my loaded standing cycle, I ran over my foot and put a hole in my ankle. A moment later, a large pickup truck drove recklessly passed me on the dusty trail. Why he was there, I have no idea. Only emergency vehicles are allowed on the narrow, undeveloped trail. This was obviously not an authorized vehicle, I thought. He almost hit me. Next, his dirt wake blew right into my face and lungs. Stories like these may be fun to recall over a pint in a pub, but they're never amusing at the time. There I was, hopping around in pain with blood pouring down my ankle into my shoe (which of course is filled with rocks), while dodging a speeding truck and choking uncontrollably from the trail dust. In my haste to fish my inhaler from my handlebar bag, just in case I couldn't catch my breath, I fell backward and landed face up with my bike and loaded panniers twisted up on top of me. Quite a sight, I'm sure.

I blew into Ohiopyle, midday, hoping to find some decent food at a nearby café or diner, somewhere near the main trailhead in town. I was almost out of water, again, as well. I couldn't leave this area without refilling. While filling both my belly and water bottles at The Firefly Grill, a group of excitable Swedish tourists circled my bike which sat, leaning against a post, just outside. They asked me tons of questions about the bike and my trip, but the most memorable part of our connection was their little girl pointing and repeating over and over with a great big grin, "No seat! No seat!" It appears my next Rolling mantra had been decided for me. Still 25 miles to go. Every little thing helps.

Near Confluence, PA, I met Carol and Mike, two locals who rolled up on me to chat. They had recognized me as the guy "rubbing his quads" back at The Firefly. They were very interested in the Mesothelioma cause and took several of my cards, pledging to donate when they returned home. Then Hans rolled down the trail and stopped between us to introduce himself. He was a true trail character. Hans rode an overloaded short wheelbase recumbent bicycle. He lived on the road most of the year, visiting trail systems all over the world. He was an eccentric Christian fundamentalist and took great pleasure in spreading the good word in his travels. After firmly speaking his mind, Hans rolled on down the trail, with conviction and an enlightened smile on his face. I wondered if I would see him again later in the week, but I never did. He was a brilliant addition to my eclectic collection of two-wheeled pilgrims.

Shortly after meeting this crew, I came upon an Ohio family who had pulled off to repair a flat bicycle tire. When I see trail trouble I always ask if help is needed, offering tools and whatever skills I have acquired through the years. They took me up on both. While assisting Mark with his tire, his wife Sarah and children Samuel and Maddie asked many questions about Mesothelioma and my route. I mentioned I had Allergic Asthma and they explained that Samuel suffered from Cystic Fibrosis. I didn't know much, at that time, about CF but I did know trouble breathing was a significant component. They taught me much about both the disease and the many direct and indirect challenges associated with it. I was touched deeply by their circumstances but could tell from Samuel's confident, knowing little smile, that he was not taking this challenge lying down and that he was tuning in to a bigger picture. Also, I could tell he was somewhat sparked by an Asthma sufferer riding hundreds of miles without sitting down while I, in turn, was greatly inspired by his attitude, strength and the positive nature of his entire family. A magical encounter, to say the least.

The last 8 miles of day 2 would jack up my heart rate past the point of comfort. I had kept a strong pace for the first 45 miles of the day, leaving little in reserve. I wasn't expecting the terrain to change much before arriving in Rockwood, my evening stop. I miscalculated. In this area, the relatively flat trail begins to track uphill a bit. Under normal circumstances, while out on a brief Sunday family ride, this wouldn't pose a problem. After riding standing all day, however, this slight grade felt more like a lengthy Rocky Mountain ascent. My heart rate began climbing as well, landing in the 140's, which for me can be risky. I knew I had to slow down but this would mean arriving at an unknown camp after dark. Also, riding this fixed-gear standing cycle slowly can feel just as tough as riding it more swiftly. Slow, stand up pedaling means more time spent working your muscles. It becomes more of an isometric activity, and your body must adjust accordingly to survive the long hours.

Just outside of Husky Haven Camp, my end of day destination, I stopped on an old trail bridge which spanned a small local river. I reflected on my day's journey and wondered what was to come later in the week. I did a short meditation to slow my heart rate and said a simple prayer of gratitude. When I had first stopped I was toast, but by the time I continued my Roll toward camp, I was energized and feeling deeply connected to every tree, breeze, and stone around me. I could not imagine a better feeling at that very moment, except for the feeling of not having to be there at all. I was there for Larry and to support a serious cause. I was there because people were suffering and I was hoping to alleviate that in some small way. Here I was basking in the beauty of that present moment. I had a feeling of joy and accomplishment so strong, that for a second, I had forgotten the truth behind both my pain and pleasure. That moment out on that bridge was truly bitter sweet.

I closed my day 2 ride at 53 miles and burned almost 5,000 kcal. I had been out on the trail for almost 11 hours. After settling with the camp office, on the other side of the river, I sorted my gear, set up my tent and camp stove, and began cooking around 8pm. I cleaned up in the dark. There were lots of spiders and mosquitoes but no time left for a defensive campfire or even a brief bike tune-up. Before calling it a night, I patched up two large blisters in the palm of my left hand and also the hole in my left ankle which I feared was heading toward infection.

There was no cell reception and no one camping close by. As I rolled up into my thin sleeping sack I could hear dogs barking and the occasional freight train in the distance. I thought about Larry, Courtney, friends and family at home, and how I'd have another 10 miles or so of "uphill" before Meyersdale, PA. My mind raced from overexertion and low blood sugar. I thought about the temperature dropping during the night. I hoped for dry weather the following day, to keep the trail firm for less rolling resistance, but if too dry the trail dust would make breathing a challenge. "What if I don't make it to D.C.? Can't control everything," I thought. "Time now to let it all go. Larry's counting on me. Do your job. Just do your best. I need to rest. Just breathe. Let go."

My Standing Cyclist trips provide me with the perfect opportunity to explore the practice of altruism or the selfless concern for the well-being of others. Considering a life of authentic compassion and kindness without a personal, self-oriented agenda. As I lay in my tent, I think, "Why am I doing this? Why am I really doing this? Do I, myself, have an agenda?" My answer, to myself, is complicated. I try to break it down into manageable chunks. First and foremost, I'm deeply compelled to impact others in a positive way. To contribute to positive change in the world. Drawn, or called, if you will. Powered by a feeling of intense correctness or primal knowing. Now, here's where things get gray and fuzzy. I love the feeling I experience from serving and giving, maybe I'm even attached to it. It feels good to push my body and my mind in an extraordinary manner. I love to ride bikes and sleep outside. Perhaps I get a rush from the uniqueness of what I do and the resulting recognition. These are two very different categories of motivation, in my opinion. The first is clearly selfless, the second could be considered quite self-oriented. So, what's the perfect blend between the two? Can there be a perfect blend? Is there really some acceptable altrustism/self'ism ratio we should strive to achieve in order to feel totally fulfilled in every way?

I admire those people who move through life modestly, doing their thing, without leaving a trace. The kind of people who make sizeable donations to a cause via a website, and when asked to leave their name and a message, they click on "anonymous". Very different from those who contribute to their local church, synagogue or hospital, in exchange for a fat front page piece in the weekly newsletter. I suppose we all wrestle with this, from time to time. We are absolutely certain our speech and intentions are righteous, but without looking deeply at this, how can we know for sure? I believe that without self-assessment, it's unlikely we'll blast apart our agendas. After all, if we can't see them, we can't address them, and when we address them, we're finally living the truth of our giving. We grow. Yes, I think of strange things lying in a tent, late at night.

I woke early that morning. Too early. The inside tent temperature had gotten down to 45 degrees during the night. Around 4am I left the comfy security of my little tent to pee, and layer up, and was soon buzzed and quite startled by a sizeable bat. I wasted no time getting back into my tent and, energized with flowing adrenaline, was compelled to remain awake and daydream about the new day and what surprises may present themselves.

Day 3 would take me from Rockwood, Pennsylvania to Spring Gap Camp in Maryland. About 43 miles into my day, I would leave the Great Allegheny Passage and begin the second leg of my multi-day journey along the C&O Canal Towpath. I would stay on that path for the next 185 miles. The balance of the ride would take me 4 days. There were still many unknowns to tackle, and up and down emotions to work through.

I swallowed hot sprouted grain cereal and sipped my hot morning green tea while huddled beneath my thin sleeping sack. There's nothing quite like the smell and texture of the cool crisp morning air on a bikepacking trip. Even the distant scent of cow was a fun and familiar experience, reminding me of past journeys through northeast farmlands and western U.S. cattle country. Mornings like these remain a favorite memory for me.

I ran into many trail riders on my third day and stopped to share info on Mesothelioma as often as possible, without cooling down too much in the process. Among those, I met Jim and Jo. Jim worked for the PA DEP near Harrisburg, PA and had, himself, been exposed to Asbestos. We spoke for quite a while and I shared Larry's Facebook page and other contact information, as I often did when the opportunity presented itself. It was exciting to see the interest and hope on the faces of those who truly connected with the topic of Mesothelioma Cancer and the Ban Asbestos cause. Their passion was intense and infectious. Moments like that helped reassure me that I was out there doing the right thing, for the right reasons. I also met and exchanged contact info with Bob near Meyersdale and Dale and Sandy near Frostburg. They were visiting from Mansfield, OH. Every human connection was invigorating, educational and inspiring. I was truly appreciating every mile. My heart didn't want the day to end. My legs had a different take on things. My body was beginning to bite back in a big way. Pains and spasms would follow my every pedal stroke for the remainder of my day.

The southeast stretch from around Deal, MD to Cumberland, MD was about 25 miles long and slightly downhill from the highest point along the GAP (2,392 feet) down through the 1/2-mile-long Big Savage Tunnel, into Cumberland. This subtle descent was still difficult for someone unable to coast. The day started out tough and would remain that way down into Spring Gap. The long dark tunnels, today and later in the week, would test both my courage and lungs. The dampness would aggravate my Allergic Asthma to a dangerous level but intentional detours were not an option.

I was noticing many recumbent bicycle tourists out on the trail. It reminded me of my own recumbent days out in Montana riding the Great Divide Mountain Bike Trail, with my friends from home. Even with the many people along this section of the route, I still felt very alone. Hours would pass as I focused on keeping my balance, my foot positions, my food/water intake, and my cadence right where they needed to be. Mindful cycling. There were times when I tuned out everything except the bike, my body and the movement. I would snap out of this when I sensed a good opportunity to discuss the Mesothelioma cause, but it wasn't always easy. There were times when seriously challenged, in most every way, that I could only think of pace and survival. The cause seemed a million miles away. It was a difficult balancing act, on many levels. It seemed like when I needed it the most, I would run into father/daughter cycling partners along the route. This synchronicity and symbolism of course, for me, represented Larry and Courtney. Sharpening up and engaging was a no brainer.

I know this will sound a little morbid but I am a big fan of cemeteries. I'm not sure why. I've always been quite comfortable around these final rest stops. Maybe it's the peaceful settings or the great historical experience of reading headstones dating back to the 1700s, or even centuries earlier in the case of Ireland's ancient burial grounds. When bike tripping or even in everyday life, I can't pass up a good cemetery and this trip was no exception. I took a break and toured the historic Pollack Cemetery not far from the Iron Mountain primitive camp. Oddly enough, the Roll through helped recharge my batteries and I soon continued on, eventually landing at my final destination of Spring Gap Camp.

After running into a man and his grandson, riding a tandem mountain bike through this semi-primitive trailside campground, I claimed my spot and started setting up camp. I'm not big on stretching, but that night I did plenty of it. My entire body was rebelling and I needed to do everything I could to avoid injury and recover swiftly including heavy duty hydration and self-massage. I hoped for an ice machine but no such luck. "This is going to be a bad one," I thought. I also had to make some light repairs to my rig. This helped keep my mind off of the bursting blisters, holes, bruises, strains and pains. It really seemed like I was falling apart.

I closed out the day at around 57 miles and clocked almost 7 hours of actual in-motion, stand-up pedaling. The good news was I had kept my average heart rate down below 120 beats per minute which was perfect. This helped keep my breathing predictable and my Allergic Asthma at bay. The bad news was, I was now positioned in between several other camps (some quite loud) pumping out smoky fires which would continue throughout the night. I laid there with my bandana around my face. It didn't really help much, so I again slept with my rescue inhaler in hand, just in case. The day's heat had taken its toll, as well. It had been running in the high 80's with only a slight occasional breeze. I now had a brutal headache which I couldn't shake. It was one of those super-sized fried evenings, where at some unknown point you shift from exhausted to high to shaky piece of shit. Wired and tired at the same time. At home, you can ride it out on the couch but out there, you're forced to deal with it. Sometimes all night, all day. Every day.

Later that evening, after calling home and also speaking with Larry for a bit, my emotions were starting to get the best of me. I got a little misty thinking about everything. I had moments of pride, then spiraled into a little self-defeat and self-pity. Then, once again, I thought of Larry and everything he was going through. I thought about his initial diagnosis, his multiple operations, and how he did not identify himself as a victim. Once again, his energy, passion for living and his activism proved to be my greatest inspiration. My inner voice-talk shifted from "I'm toast. I'm suffering. I can't do this any-more," to "Suck it up you woosy. Think of what Larry is going through. This is a freakin' vacation for you. This isn't real life. Give it all you've got and more. It's the least you can do." A sobering self-chat.

I christened day 4 by falling out of an outhouse. It could have been worse I suppose. I could have fell in. After regaining my composure, I was happy to discover that the AA battery powered field charger I brought on this trip successfully charged my smartphone to 55%, sufficient for another full riding day providing I keep it powered off except when truly needed. On a trip like this, conservation of energy on every level is important, I thought.

I met some of my neighbors while tearing down camp. It was interesting to connect with the threesome of women campers who provided me with loud, sometimes tense, entertainment from the night before. Now more subdued, they groggily stumbled around camp mumbling about who is doing what, with little interest in chatting with this traveling cyclist about the cause or anything else for that matter.

Beyond some typical lack of sleep symptoms, I was feeling good after awakening but soon developed a tight, queasy stomach. Immediately I thought about the wells I had been drawing water from throughout the tour. I was told by a fellow camper that they were shocked regularly for purification and I wondered if I had been consuming too much chlorine or other chemicals and now I was beginning to pay the price. My stomach worsened.

I sat back for a bit before heading out, to give my belly some time to recover but it was slow going. As I laid curled up near my loaded bike, memories of dreams from the last several nights came to me. That night before, I had a vivid dream/memory of my father and his work injury that removed him from the workforce at a fairly young age. The dream played out in a way that showed me how important that one event actually was, within the larger context of our lives. If he hadn't been injured, would he have remained a welder working around Asbestos and other dangerous contaminants? Would we have been indirectly exposed, as a result, like many family members are? Would I have grown up in New York City rather than in upstate New York where I learned to work and play in the natural world? In my dream, I kept hearing the phrase, "Everything happens for a reason".

Some say we choose the circumstances of our birth and incarnate specifically for one or more reasons, for soul growth, and that represents our path or Dharma. The truth of our lives. A flow that is fueled by both free will and determinism, together in concert. A daily balance between the cosmic crossroads laid out before us and the choice we make in every moment. The choice of which path to take, at every intersection. As I held my stomach, sweating, suffering, I wondered how my dad, mom and I all fit together in the bigger picture. I thought about why this pain inside was slowing me down this particular morning. Was it to remove me from a harmful convergence of events later in the day? Or perhaps it was placing me right where I needed to be, to support my efforts. Maybe this delay would align me with some important person further into my week. Perhaps someone in need of my connection, or someone I need to connect with. Is this that same synchronicity that Carl Yung spoke of almost a century ago?

As quickly as it arrived, my discomfort faded away and I was back out on the trail for my 4th day of standing cycling. It was a crisp 50-degree morning and the temperature and scenery reminded me of my Lake Champlain tour. I was drawing energy from everything around me. The breeze, the trees and other features in nature. Brilliant, elegant, inviting elements surrounding and encouraging me to not just jump down onto pedals that drive a mechanical device, but to flow smooth with a smile, with every stroke and every breath. It was a soothing and inviting feeling I hadn't quite experienced before. Not a high but a balance and intense clarity. A balance of energy expended and energy received. It was perfect. All was just right. Even the morning's trail dust and burnt brake scent from the nearby railroad could not blur my perception. It was as if I was no longer riding a bike. For several hours that day, I was simply witnessing the riding of a bike. I just happened to be in the right place at the right time to capture this special viewpoint. I just showed up. I was so connected that I was disconnected, or was it the other way around? Either way, it felt fantastic.

My floating, perfect pedal stroking continued for what must have been 2 hours before a technical change in terrain woke me from my trance. My eyes sent a wakeup call up to my brain. "Sharpen your focus. See the trail. Read your body. Course corrections required." When I ride my fixed gear standing cycle off-road, I am always conflicted. My multi-geared, freewheel, mountain bike roots tell me to plow through challenging lines with confidence. You have the bike to handle it. But when standing on a bike that cannot coast, with a relatively high center of gravity, panniers, skinny tires and no suspension, I need to lean my mindset toward survival. I need to avoid, not conquer. Stable lines must be picked, every moment, to maintain balance and a steady pace. The switch happens fast and automatically. It's great fun, but unforgiving. One small mistake and you go over forward or take a heavy spinning pedal to the shin at full speed. My sharpened pedal spikes intended to keep my feet firmly in place, especially important when standing up, can become your worst enemies if you blink out for even a moment.

Tunnel time. About 20 miles into my day it was time to explore the Paw Paw tunnel. I had heard about this 3,118-foot-long, dark, damp tunnel from other trail riders. I was both looking forward to it and dreading it. As I made my approach, I pulled off the trail to fish my headlamp from my handlebar pack and mounted it securely beneath my helmet. As soon as I rode through the entrance the temperature dropped significantly and my eyes began their adjustment from bright sunlight to the dim beam from my headlamp. To my right was a rough, brick lining and to my left was a thin wooden handrail which separated riders or hikers from the black canal waters below. You could almost smell and taste the history within this tunnel. You could practically see and feel the people who both built and used this passageway to travel through the rugged mountain terrain. Soon after entering the tunnel, my energy suddenly became depleted and my breathing labored. My chest tightened and my hands clenched the grips of my handlebars. There were no other people in the tunnel and I hadn't seen another person on the trail for hours. I felt very isolated, like on the surface of a dark, distant moon. My legs felt wiry and weak as I became keenly aware of what I was doing. By standing up, riding this sort of bike through this narrow dark space, I had to be perfectly accurate in my stroke and steering. A little to the left or right and I would surely crash. The fear factor was upped as I realized that by standing up, I was much higher than the guardrail with a clear view into the canal. A decent 10-foot drop. That said, I was still enjoying myself and working through my fear and my breathing challenges until..."the message".

I am not one to be easily spooked, as my friends and family can attest to, but Paw Paw tunnel definitely made its mark on me. About halfway through the over 1/2-mile tunnel, the darkness is at its deepest. There is no breeze, the air feels dead and the walls feel like they are closing in around you. As I Rolled forward carefully, looking several feet ahead of me with each pedal stroke, I saw a large word written with liquid across the narrow trail surface, "HELP". I immediately stopped, scraping my right shoulder against the abrasive tunnel wall. I couldn't believe what I was seeing. How could this be here, I thought. Then my logical side jumped in, and I reasoned that someone who came through ahead of me that morning must have done it to spook those who would come through later in the day. It could have been done using a squirt from a water bottle or even a urine stream. Then I got off the bike and examined the lettering more carefully. That's when the spook factor increased. Each letter was incredibly sharp and perfectly formed. This was not a joker peeing out the word on a dark, narrow path and a water bottle squirt could not have crisply crafted what I was seeing. I glanced over the railing to the left of this word to make sure no one was truly in distress and called out several times. My stomach dropped and my legs weakened. My energy almost entirely left my body. I knew I had to get out of that tunnel right away, no screwing around. I jumped back on the bike and hastily launched myself up and forward at a steady, speedy pace until I cleared the far end of the tunnel and fell back out into the sunlight. At that point, I felt very ill.

Soon after leaving the darkness of the narrow path, I dropped my bike near a well site and sat back against the well pump, unable to think clearly or move with any significant strength. I would say I was panicked or that my blood sugar was low, but that wasn't the case. My heart rate was lower than usual, my breathing slow and steady and I had eaten shortly before entering the tunnel. In truth, I could not explain what was going on with me. I have been hypothermic before, so I know that was not what I was experiencing. I even lacked the energy to swing the well pump handle to replenish my water supply. I recall wanting to do a brief meditation and ground myself but could not focus my mind on any one thing. My brain was scrambled and linty. It was as if something had sucked the life out of me. This lasted about 30 minutes and passed rather suddenly. I was up and Rolling at 100% before I knew it. I had never experienced anything like that and haven't since. I still cannot explain it, and try not to think about it too often. It still gives me the willies. As I Rolled off, feeling strong, I looked down to find a huge, beautiful feather. It brought me great pleasure, for reasons I also cannot explain. Another mystery worth mentioning.

As I approached Little Orleans, echoes of distant gunshots grew louder, competing with the sounds of my hungry stomach. Time for some lunch, I thought. I swung into the first establishment I could find which, as it turned out, was a local biker (motorcycle) bar. As I sat at the bar waiting for my sandwiches to be prepared, I couldn't help notice the numerous posters of bikini clad women hung along the walls surrounding the pool table and behind the bartender. A pleasant surprise at this phase of my trip, I must say. I sat back and thought about my old road cycling, or roadie, days when friends and I would innocently stop at roughneck bars like this for water and snacks in the middle of long day rides, wearing our shiny road tights and colorful bike jerseys, turning many heads but not in a good way. Glad those days are long gone. Now, my trip attire has me looking more like a hiker or hobo and less like a Tour de France competitor, which in addition to being quite comfortable makes me far more approachable to locals and helps support meaningful, down-to-earth conversations. This local bar crowd was no exception and my brief break there was both enjoyable and memorable. I met many good people, all of which were very interested in my trip and the cause behind it.

I wrapped up the day at an isolated, primitive camp site called White Rock. It was a 90-degree day and I was out there for almost 10 hours. I came in just shy of 50 miles and maintained an average heart rate of only 111 BPM. I was very pleased with how things turned out and looked forward to completing my camp chores, journaling my progress, and kicking back to view the clear sky and glow of the stars. I considered my body which was faring better than expected at this stage of the trip. Left knee pain. Right Achilles tendon ache. Slight headache. Lungs open. Right wrist slight sprain. Overall, very good. I reflected on my near mystical experiences. On all the positive occurrences, and disturbing incidents as well. I was very thankful for everything and was compelled to pray and reflect under the stars. I once again thanked the universe for the abilities and opportunities I had been graced with, and focused positively on success for the sake of Larry and everyone else involved in this endeavor.

I felt especially connected to the natural world around me. Hypersensitive. I heard every bird, every frog, and the movement of the trees in every breeze. I felt the cool air flow, the hardpack crunch of the campsite ground beneath my feet, and picked up the sweet scent of this collective Earth. A wonderfully calm evening at the close of a tumultuous day. I thought about the beautiful feather I had found at my feet en route to Little Orleans. Not the last I would find on that trip. I experienced many things that day and learned much about who I had been and who I was becoming. I liked what I was seeing. It fit like a well-worn cap, carefully conditioned over many years of use. It simply felt, correct.

Lying in my tent, my brain drifted away from the contemplative to the mechanical. I had discovered earlier in the day that my rear wheel, which is attached to my frame via two big nuts, needed to be shifted backward. My chain had stretched from the ongoing force of pedaling while standing up. I had brought a wrench with me for this purpose but in the field it had proven useless. I would need to explore Hancock the following day to find a more robust tool and spare batteries as well. I also needed to find additional clean water. I had made the poor decision to dump known potable water thinking this primitive site would have more for my refill, but it proved to be too rusty to drink.

Perhaps the most important thing I considered while lying there was my rendezvous with Larry and Courtney on my last day. This would have to time out just right. Perhaps Larry could run the 5 miles toward me as I approached D.C., and when we connected, Larry could turn around and run the 5 miles alongside me back into the city for our photo-shoot with Courtney and Mesothelioma Applied Research Foundation representative, Danielle, who planned to meet us three at the endpoint of the trip. I (very) briefly wondered if Larry would be up for a 10 mile run in his current condition. Certainly, Larry wouldn't be a problem. If he decided to do it, he would do it. I should be more concerned with my own perseverance and ability. After all, this had never been done before and I had many miles yet to go. Would I be able to deliver?

Before falling asleep I spoke with my mother, who remains one of my great teachers and "teachings" in life, who assured me that I had what it took to get the job done. I needed that call more than I think she realized. That night I dreamt about the United States and the freedom we value so highly. In the dream, people were telling me and Larry we couldn't and shouldn't do certain things. I remember in the dream feeling like - here we all are talking about freedom to be and do whatever we want, but most of us don't exercise that very freedom. We just keep doing the same things over and over, complaining we're bored and depressed. Unfulfilled. Without any real adventure in our lives. Rarely pushing passed our own boundaries. We are truly an odd species.

That night was relatively uneventful with the exception of some (hip) hot spots caused by my overinflated sleeping pad. It turned out to be a bizarre little adventure in its own right and contained similar learned lessons picked up from my "dollar and the pen" experience years before.

There I was lying there in the dark envisioning the little black knob I know I must reach for and turn in order to release a bit of air from my sleeping pad, but can't. I'm stuck, I thought. I can't just lie here all night uncomfortable but I can't move a single exhausted muscle to improve my world. In retrospect it sounds kind of comical to refer to something seemingly minor as major, but believe me, at that moment the frustration and pain were Earth shattering in my own little mind. Funny how we perceive things when we're down and nearly out. It often seems so much worse that it really is. Just then something clicked and I gained the gumption to reach out through the darkness and grab hold of this liberating piece of plastic and began turning. Well, I tried turning it anyway, but with no luck. My fatigued fingers slipped right around the slick little surface. Another brutal setback, I thought, of course blowing this way out of proportion. I was borderline delirious and so annoyed that I let out a long, robust moan. Luckily no one was around for many miles.

Soon I crossed over from struggle to gallant quest. Time to get creative, I thought. This little knob is not going to cost me a good night's sleep. I decided to calm down and focus on solving this seemingly hopeless problem while in my goofy, hypnagogic state of mind. After a painfully long pause, I remembered that I had a small rubber band wrapped around my MP3 player, exactly why I don't know, but it was there just the same. I reached around groggily in the dark, found that thin little savior, and twisted it around the knob, just like those rubber grips you open tightly sealed peanut butter jars with. With one jerk, air began to flow out, just enough to ease the pressure on my hip. Success! Well, not exactly. I guess I let a little too much air out and now could feel the many tiny, sharp rocks poking up through the floor of my bivy tent. This was catastrophic, I thought. I wanted to cry until I began laughing at myself and my silly little plight. Another sweet little teaching on the path to D.C. Never take your situation or yourself too seriously. There's always a way and things are never as bad as they seem.

Day 5, only 3 days left to go. Arose early, 5am. After washing up my camp pot with the nasty well water I had discovered the night before, I headed out onto the trail around 7:30am and Rolled right up to another feather greeting me as I started off. It was beautifully striped, maybe an owl feather, I wasn't sure. I had been thinking about my own personal concept of heaven just before seeing it, felt a chill, and made a mental note as I Rolled on. It was a good feeling and I hoped to remember it as my trip progressed.

I road into Hancock, MD to make my purchases and mingle at a local bike shop. By now, I should be used to the mixed reception I sometimes receive when connecting with traditional cyclists both on the trail and in shops, but I'm still not 100% ok with it, to this day. These guys had no interest whatsoever in what I was doing and why I was doing it. I tried explaining about Larry and Mesothelioma, and how I was standing to raise awareness but all I got back was a blank look and a mellow "ok". Needless to say, I didn't stay long and decided to head off to the local hardware store for the wrench I needed to adjust my rear wheel and chain tension.

When I was done in Hancock I headed down through Licking Creek where I met Tom and Alisha who were riding the trail before heading off to a family funeral. Everyone copes with loss in different ways. They chose to start this difficult day on two wheels, in nature. A good way, I would say. It was a pleasure connecting with them, but I had one regret. It had become quite hot, almost 90 degrees, and I was feeling the heat in a big way. As we parted ways, my brainless last words were an overly and unnaturally positive, "Have a great day guys!" They raised their eyebrows and smiled politely as they cycled off in the opposite direction. I shrunk back into my standing pace and muddled on, feeling like an idiot. Blame it on the heat, I thought. Blame it on the heat.

Just before Williamsport, MD, I needed to make a trailside porta potty stop and decided to use the time to change into my shorts. My legs were roasting. The agile me had it covered but, once again, the klutzy me had other porta potty plans on that hot, humid day. Plans that included flailing, falling and hitting my head on the door. Eventually I made it out, but was now sporting a rich new cologne that resembled one-part cow, one-part chicken and one part which remains unidentifiable to me to this day. Without any water, I continued on as-is hoping to avoid any close contact until the next creek was available. Apparently, I need to stay far away from porta potties, I thought.

I am always moved deeply by the homeless, but especially when bike tripping. Run-ins remind me that I am out there, unshowered, hungry, worn out and alone, by choice. That I can return to my home whenever I wish and that home will be inviting and comfortable. After passing by a beautiful dam along a narrow section of trail, I came upon a homeless man and his bicycle. At first I thought he was simply touring but soon it became clear that the goods overloading his beaten up backpack and bike bags were all he had in this world. It appeared as if his bike was his best friend and the natural world around him was his home. I asked him if he needed anything, one cyclist to another. He avoided eye contact with me and sheepishly responded with a quiet "no". I caught a strong vibe from him. A combination of shame, exhaustion, fear, and a deep sense of sadness. As I approached him I picked up a strong scent of urine and feces, and I could see his hands and face were dirty and slightly bruised, with scabs scattered about. I deeply wished I could help him. I imagined paying for a hotel, getting him showered up and fed, and maybe buying him some new gear for proper touring. I asked again if I could do anything for him. This time, he seemed surprised by my willingness to chat and actually approach him. I made a few jokes to make him feel at ease and we made some small talk. Very small. He cracked a slight smile but still focused his glance a bit off-center. He wasn't offering up any information. Just then, the subtle energy I was reading transitioned from shyness to agitation, even belligerence.

This man was clearly not accustomed to a stranger taking an interest in his well-being and didn't know what to do. He began moving side to side uncomfortably. I knew my presence and words were not helping as I had hoped they would, and swiftly planned my exit. I wished him well and Rolled off down the trail. He seemed pleased to see me go. He was alone again, left only with Mother Nature and his trusty steed. I never knew his name but was compelled to call him Jim in my memories and in a few post-trip dreams. Jim's energy stayed with me for many miles. I could not help compare him and I, on that day. Our scent, dirty clothing, hunger, exhaustion from the heat, and our isolation from others, all somewhat similar. Each one of us was only one step away from being the other. It was the difference of one decision, or illness, or act of God that separated us and our paths. Or were we really that separate, I thought. Isn't everyone and everything part of the same bigger picture? In any case, I was grateful for having met him and grateful for my own life in a new, much deeper way.

The day before, I had begun noticing a rash around the area of my right Achilles tendon. It was now noticeable on my left as well. I was hoping it wasn't poison ivy or anything like that. If it was to get infected, it would surely slow me down, I thought. It was 92 degrees in the shade and these irritations were burning badly. Of all the items I had in my little first aid kit, I lacked anything for rashes or burns. The closest thing I had was an antibacterial cream so I stopped to apply some to both areas. I could see from my map that a sizeable, forced detour was coming up. I packed up my kit and returned to the trail, hoping to minimize lost time and get to my next primitive campsite before dark.

The detour was a 6-mile road ride that, for a traditional touring cyclist on an ordinary day, would have been a snap. But I was by no means traditional and the day was searing hot. The hills and exposure proved to be tougher than I had expected. No coasting and one fixed-gear, with a full load, was zapping my energy faster than I could recuperate. The heat was radiating down from the sky and up from the pavement, sandwiching my pale almost translucent legs and arms in between. Even with sunscreen on, I was beginning to burn. I found myself stopping along these 6 miles more than I would have liked. I even walked my bike up one short, steep hill, carefully avoiding my spiked pedal which rotates as all fixed gear bikes roll forward.

At 4:30pm I was still on the roadway detour and my handlebar bag thermometer, while sitting in an open pocket out of direct sunlight, read just over 95 degrees. The usual pounding in my head when overexerting myself grew much louder until that's all I could focus on. My eyes became pools of stinging sweat. My water and electrolyte powder were running low and my legs were giving out. I slipped into a field for a quick pee break and both legs were shaking so badly that I almost relieved myself...on myself. Hobbling back to my bike, which was leaning down on its side at the edge of the road, my legs stopped working altogether and I fell over into the gravel. Almost there, I thought. Just a few more miles, don't stop now, you're almost back onto the trail where you'll be nestled beneath, at least some, tree cover.

Shortly after getting back to the main route, I came upon Big Woods primitive campsite. I was thrilled to stop for the night, rest and rehydrate, until I found the well water in that camp to be just as rusty as the previous night's. I fell back, broken. The next primitive site, and water well, was about 3 miles further down the trail but I had nothing left in me to give. I sat on the ground at Big Woods and watched my quad muscles spasm, for entertainment, until I was distracted by a couple of rowdy locals emerging from the woods, crossing the main trail. They were staggering around hollering about their lost pickup truck, both of them obviously loaded, and offered me chunks of barbecued hog. They disappeared as quickly as they turned up. I thought it was a dream. Maybe it was. Eventually I found enough strength to pick up my rig and continue on. It was not a pretty 3 miles. I almost slipped off the trail several times. My concentration was weakened, and when riding that bike in that manner, that meant injury was eminent. I had to snap out of it fast and focus or I'd soon have one of many passing tree trunks tattooed across my fore-head, along with a mouthful of local dirt for dinner.

It must have taken me an hour to go those last few miles. I landed at Horseshoe Bend camp well before sunset and was greeted by yet another feather on the ground right in front of my tent space. A faint smile peeked out from behind my grimace. I closed the day with almost 52 miles behind me. I had been on the trail for over 10 hours. With the high heat, I was sure I was dehydrated. I hadn't urinated much throughout the day and when I did, my output was much darker than it should have been. Both are good indications of dehydration. As I was setting up camp, two more feathers appeared on the ground, side by side, between my tent and a neighboring tree. Very nice, I thought, still wondering if there was a bigger meaning behind these sightings or were they just ordinary remnants of balding birds.

I had a quick and simple meal then settled in my tent for some shuteye, but not before peeing awkwardly around the perimeter of my camp. After sunset I had been hearing many rather robust noises in the brush surrounding my primitive site. With no one else around for many miles I knew I had some critter neighbors and wanted to discourage any shenanigans. I had no idea if my pee plan would do any good, but in my End of Days stupor it seemed like a good idea. It must have been an odd sight to see. My legs were barely working and my balance was shot. I had quite a stagger going while conducting business.

As I laid back on top of my sleeping pad I could hear, of all things, music! At first, I thought the day's heat had me hallucinating but then I saw lights flashing through my thin tent wall. It was a passing party boat, far off in the distance, with Joan Jett karaoke blasting from its upper deck. I hadn't realized how close I was to the water's edge but with no docks or trails leading ashore, I was safely tucked away from the action and soon fell fast asleep. Around 4am, the day's trail dust caught up with me and my breathing, or lack of, woke me with a short burst of adrenaline and a small dose of panic. I took a moment to regain control over my emotions and eventually my airflow. As I shifted my position in my tight little tent, I realized how much my knees, ankles, and Achilles tendons were hurting. I laid there for over an hour considering how I could reconfigure my body position while Rolling, and if loosening my laces on my left shoe would help. I was troubleshooting when I should have been recovering. I would pay for that within hours when I would once again hit the trail to begin my 6th, and next to last day, of my Standing Cyclist Mesothelioma Challenge.

I stumbled out of my tent at sunrise, slipped on my shirt and grabbed some chow before wrapping up camp chores. It was a crisp, cool morning and I hoped it would remain that way. My body was still fried from yesterday's sun. Before taking off, I made myself some green tea and thought about Antietam Battlefield which sat only minutes south of my camp. I had complex, chaotic dreams during the night but could not recall any specific details. I wondered if they included visits from restless souls. Many people lost their lives during the infamous Civil War battle at Antietam and I had been sleeping in their backyard. Near ground zero. In a single day, on September 17, 1862, over 20,000 men were wounded, killed or went missing. In the weeks that followed, many more died from their wounds and from various diseases. The quiet, nearby village of Sharpsburg was transformed into a makeshift trauma center and burial ground which extended for many miles in every direction, including my direction. My heart hurt for those men and their loved ones. It was a sad and brutal war, and Antietam was a particularly brutal battle. Chills moved down my spine. I wondered if I was sitting in the company of killers and angels.

As I tore down camp, I noticed the two feathers, that had sat alongside my tent just hours before, were now gone. But not entirely. As I rolled my gear up to the sign which labeled my site location, just below the trail itself, I found both feathers slipped neatly behind the rough little sign. The sign was supported by a tall post which rose at least six feet up from the ground. There was one feather on each end, pointing up to the sky. I could not explain this. Yet another chill ran down my spine. There were no feathers on that signpost the night before and, yes, these were in fact the same feathers I had seen on the ground. I could tell from several distinguishing features. What was the likelihood that someone was hiking through my isolated camp in the middle of the night, walked around my tent in the dark, found the feathers and placed them up on that sign and in that very position? Had I gotten my answer about Antietam? Did I have company?

The early morning trail was laced with spider webbing strung across, for many miles. For anyone uncomfortable around spiders, this is not the best way to start your day. Luckily I'm not one of those people, although I did freak out a couple of times when I thought I had inhaled a few. After pedaling through the jungle of webs for several hours, I came upon an old timer on his morning walk near Sheperdstown. He appeared rugged, athletically built, and moved swiftly for his years. It was now quite humid and my breathing was being affected. Neither the growing heat nor high humidity appeared to slow him down in any way. We both stopped to chat. After pumping me for info about my purpose out on the trail and why I was standing on a bike that doesn't coast, he skeptically eyed my puny legs and rear rack and asked, "So, what keeps you from sitting down on that thing when no one's around?" I explained that loaded with gear, I was already far exceeding the weight limit for both the light-duty rack and its 2 small mounting bolts. I could practically wiggle the rack with my hands. Sitting on that thin piece of aluminum, lightly supported and already overloaded, would be pointless. I would end up on the ground in seconds. Besides, I explained, even if it held me, it would place me in a less efficient, uncomfortable and awkward peddling position. I wouldn't get very far. He countered with, "Well, you could do it going downhill at least, to save energy. Just sit and coast with your weight mostly on your pedals." Of course, this theory held no water once I reiterated the fact that the rack cannot support my bodyweight and that I cannot coast on this bike. The pedals are always rotating. Finally, he tipped his cap and smiled which I took as, at least, his willingness to understand. We continued to chat for a bit before going our separate ways. By the end, he was a believer. That wasn't the first time my ability to ride and tour standing for long distances was questioned and I knew it wouldn't be the last. After all, how strong can a pair of chicken legs be? In time, every cyclist discovers that true strength and endurance come from within and has little to do with muscle, bone and fancy riding gear.

On my way toward Harpers Ferry, I was passing by the southernmost point of the Antietam battlefield region, and hadn't yet seen any ghostly apparitions. Honestly, at this point in the trip, I was more concerned with the living. I began running into some strange characters and suddenly found myself shy and even guarded. Also, there were caves along this section of trail and my mind began to play tricks on me. I would catch a shadow near a cave entrance and mistaken it for a person peering out at me, as I rode by. Then, more breathing troubles. Trail dust was kicking up into the hot, humid air. My swift pace, poor sleep and general anxiety from this odd, isolated environment was spiking my heart rate. I needed to calm down and slow down. I think I was moving faster than normal to beat the high afternoon heat, but that obviously wasn't working. I felt like I was suffocating. I reached down beneath my shirt and quickly snapped off my heart rate monitor transmitter strap, which wrapped snugly around my chest. What normally felt comfortable and even cozy, now felt like I had a truck parked across my chest. At that point, I had little concern over my exact beats per minute and how many calories I was burning. I just wanted to breathe in and out with as little restriction as possible. I even took off my helmet, which is something I never do. I am a huge advocate for brain buckets. I've had too many close calls myself and heard of far too many serious head injuries that could have been easily avoided with the use of a helmet.

Funny how things time out. As I was trying to keep it together and not keel over, I ran into a hiker named Jill. She was an HR professional by training, a glowing positive person and very interested in the purpose behind my trip. I answered many of her questions about Asbestos exposure and Mesothelioma, or at least tried to, in my shaky state. She had a calming, healing presence and although I cannot recall her face today, her essence remains. Jill explained how she was recovering from a very serious mountain bike crash and was interested in bicycle touring on the C&O trail as part of her recovery. I believe we are often given exactly what we need, just at the right moment in time. Reflecting back, I needed Jill to help remind me of the deep meaning and importance far beneath my surface challenges. Perhaps she needed to run into me, as well.

As I approached Harpers Ferry, I could see the huge foot bridge that rose high above the Potomac. As I stared up the long metal trailside staircase, I leaned back against my loaded bike, almost falling over. I was low on energy and was now in pain from my neck down to my ankles. My muscles were tired, weak and very shaky. I could barely grip items with my hands. My fingers were not closing properly. My head began to spin and I had to sit down. I opened my handlebar pack where I typically store my phone, compass, knife, a few energy bars and several special little items such as my dad's old leather keychain and a little Woolworth's photograph of my grandpa and me when I was about 6, shortly before his passing. I pulled out the pic and touched his face. I could almost smell his old brown leather jacket and hat. In his younger days, he was a wanderer, moving man, and sometimes a hellraiser, but always a loyal, loving force of nature. He had a kind energy about him. I needed that energy now, I thought. A healing energy. I drew it from my grandfather, from my father and from the many supporters of that trip including people like Jill. Above all, I drew it from Larry and Courtney. I was not far from D.C. I thought about how terrible it would be to fail, this close to reaching our goal. I mustered up enough mental energy to lock up my bike and panniers on a trailside rack and enough leg power to climb up over the bridge into Harpers Ferry for some food and drink. I stumbled through the streets like a drunk, limping slowly from sidewalk to sidewalk. I picked up some sandwiches and sports drink at a little Cafe run by a young stoner dude. At first, he thought I was injured. Then he thought I was homeless. At that point, I resembled both, and couldn't blame him for his assumptions.

The food didn't help much, but I had to continue on. I was once again questioning myself and feeling afraid. Afraid of injury, being alone, afraid of failure. Even afraid of fear. I had no room for this right now, I thought. I needed to once again dig in, as I had back in Ireland along Connor Pass and in Iceland across the treacherous Snaefellsnes Peninsula. I had to refocus and get serious about why I was out there. Real serious. As I went to unlock my bike, I saw another feather sitting nearby that wasn't there when I left 40 minutes earlier. I took that as an approval of my vulnerability and good intentions. I was soon back on the bike.

At 2:14pm in the afternoon, I fell into the most exquisite performance zone I had ever experienced, to date. My rhythm was perfectly balanced. Balanced breathing and movement. I was still weak and in pain, but I simply watched it all and accepted it as part of this journey, and I continued on...and on. I had a Rolling marathon of 26 miles left in the day before I could bed down for the night. I was headed to the Horse Pen primitive campsite, which sat yet another Rolling marathon distance away from D.C. and my final destination where I would meet up with Larry Davis. Where we would travel into the city side by side, for the cause. "Got to keep Rolling," I kept repeating to myself. Over and over, mile after mile, until finally reaching my camp around 5:30pm.

I literally fell into camp which, much like all the other primitive sites on this trip, were small single, sometimes double tent sites nestled tightly between several trees. There were zero amenities except a simple water well with a heavy steel pump handle. As I sat in the dirt, I began to evaluate my condition but was so gone I lost interest and I think consciousness for a few moments. When I regained at least some focus, I thought about the people I had met that day. I recognized I had ridden almost 60 miles, standing without coasting. I thought about many things, all flashing through my brain at lightning speed. I thought about calling home, calling Larry to finalize our plans for our last day, and about the huge tree which sat in the middle of the site. It appeared to be very old. I wondered if it was around during the Civil War. It must have experienced many remarkable things in its day. Both positive and negative. Peace and trauma. I drifted to sleep for a while sitting up, with my face in my hands. I know I dreamt but, once again, I could remember little.

As I struggled to set up my tent and fire up my camp stove, I had a little ladybug land on my hand. It was the first I had seen all week. I let her ride along as I completed my chores. The blisters on my hands made each simple little chore extra difficult. Breathing moved passed "difficult" to a whole new level for me. I was now too tired to breathe. Too tired to even care to breathe.

With regards to the trip, I was letting go, as much as possible, without shutting down and off altogether. Recognizing and accepting the "what if" thoughts, and releasing the fear. All of it. I was close to actually pulling this thing off, I thought. I was so close I could hear and see the airplanes overhead coming from and heading to Dulles Airport. Larry was just down the road and I would soon be traveling next to him. I was only one Rolling marathon away from accomplishing something I could never have imagined accomplishing several years back when I couldn't breathe well enough to take out the garbage. Now, not only was I physically bouncing back, I was clearing out much of the trash in my head and heart. There is nothing quite like being broken down, to help you build back up again stronger than ever. I was going to get to the end tomorrow morning, I thought. Nothing was going to stop me.

Before bed, Beth and Paul rolled into my camp and would give me even more to think about. Beth was an Architect and Paul was an Engineer. Together, they were a very practical couple. Their questions focused mostly on my career choices and my ability to take time off for a week long charity adventure. They didn't seem to "get me" but I did get them. They were me, a decade ago. Before my father passed. Before my Allergic Asthma diagnosis. They were sharp and edgy, highly confident, a bit quirky, driven, a little sarcastic with a touch of passive-aggressive thrown in for good measure. Life changes in waves and we were clearly surfing different breaks, but no matter. These were good people and upon my return home, one of my favorite email messages was from Beth. Her encouraging words were a pleasant surprise. After chatting for a while in camp, I hit the bivy round 8pm. I was going to need a decent night's sleep to wrap things up the next day. I needed brain power not simply leg power. I would be interviewed for a video which would be used to further the cause well after our endeavor was over. I had to make sense.

I checked in with my team at home, before fading off to dream land. There were troubles back in PA that worried me. My family could use my help, but I wasn't there. I wanted to control that, but I knew, given my location and mode of transportation, and my mission here, that would not be realistic. They had it covered, but in my head, I felt I should have been doing more to help. I considered this while curled up cozy in my bivy. What I picked up on was important. "You can't always be the Project Manager or hero. You can't always have all the answers. Always wanting and needing to be the problem solver is part ego." Ah, there's that word again, ego, I thought. Next thought, no thought. Just snoring. Enough trailside spirituality for the day.

I woke much earlier than my camp mates, and Rolled on out toward our nation's Capital before 6:30am. I had spoken with both Larry and Courtney the previous night, to sort out our final details. Larry would be entering the trail around milepost 3 and would begin running in my direction. We hoped to connect around milepost 5. We would then continue on together into the city, where we would meet up with Courtney who, as a media professional, would film our arrival. Myself on the bike, with Larry running alongside.

I spent most of my riding time that morning trying to pace myself properly, to arrive just in time to align with Larry, as planned. This, at times involved unexpected standing sprints which further taxed my already impaired physiology, but it was all well worth it. The moment I saw Larry, I knew we had done it. We weren't even in the city yet, but his smile and warm greeting filled the energy void I had been suffering from for days, and the pain was no more. I was now fully engaged, not for myself, but for this man who had flown here from Florida just to meet me and run by my side for the cause. His cause. A man whose suffering was deep, but whose strength was boundless. A dying man whose remaining years were being spent informing and assisting others afflicted with his man-made Cancer. Many of these people were too weak to learn, engage, and fight, so Larry did it for them. Here I was, a small man Rolling towards The Capitol city of the United States of America alongside a real hero. A big man, in both stature and essence. What little of "me" that remained, faded further away at that moment. I was a minuscule piece of a grand endeavor and I was honored to be just that, and no more. This began as a Standing Cyclist project but was ending as an epic teaching. A humbling instance of tribute and service. An authentic use of ability and opportunity to serve others. A chilling series of moments.

As we came off the trail together and entered the busy city streets of Washington D.C., Courtney was there to capture the moment of our arrival, as expected. Once we settled to a stop, she began interviewing and filming Larry, myself and Danielle from the Mesothelioma Applied Research Foundation. The piece was posted on the internet and continues to touch people close to the cause, to this day. When the formalities were behind us, Larry grabbed my standing fixed-gear bike, jumped on and began flying down the busy D.C. city streets, this time with me running alongside him. Most people need time to get comfortable on my standing cycles, but not Larry. The natural athlete that he was, he picked it up almost immediately. As I ran, the pain and grime of the last 7 days fell from my mind. I could think only of the joy and excitement on his face as he peddled my bizarre bicycle. He was simply having fun. In the midst of turmoil and tragedy in his world, he remained positive and curious like a big kid. People like Larry are born, contribute, and die every day. Some are recognized and inspire the rest of us to perform and persevere. We find courage and gain strength from people like this. What we do with that courage and strength is up to us.

We all walked over to the local bicycle shop together, where I shipped my bike back home to PA, then we all stopped in at the world famous Georgetown Cupcake for a quick snack. Later on, Larry, Courtney and I capped the day off with some stellar Mexican food further down the street. After a week of camp food and energy bars, this truly hit the spot. Finally, it was time to say our goodbyes. I gave Larry a huge hug and thanked him and Courtney for believing in me. I could tell from his body language, he wasn't expecting a hug and was maybe a little uncomfortable, emotionally. He held back a bit, although it could have been due to my trail grime. Either way, I understood. That day was the first and last time I would see Larry Davis in person. Within 2 years of our Mesothelioma Challenge, Larry would pass on.

Shortly after Larry left for the airport, Courtney and I parted ways. I would take over the room at the Inn they had stayed at the previous night, but not before wandering the streets of D.C. to both clear my head and place everything that had just happened into perspective. I found myself in an Irish pub, sharing trail stories and information about the cause. I found it ironic that here, many miles and years after my Ireland ride, I am once again celebrating a successful trip surrounded by warm people and rich pints of Guinness. But this time was different. My head was different, and my heart was surely not the same heart that set out from Pittsburgh one week earlier. After tossing back a few cold ones and calling home to check in, I drifted to DuPont Circle. I sat and people-watched for over an hour, trying to adjust from isolation to crowded city. It would take many weeks to fully adjust. To realign my senses, brain, body and soul.

The next morning after my first night's sleep in a real bed, I made my way to the bus station. My trip wasn't over yet. I needed to make my way back to Pittsburgh, where my car safely sat awaiting my arrival, hopefully. Waiting for the bus, I met many good people on their own magical journey, including Stephanie from northern England. She was a born traveler who was in the middle of a full U.S. tour, before heading back home to college. We shared stories about our various adventures and the Meso cause. As I sat on the bus that afternoon, I found it a little unnerving that I could not feel either one of my big toes, with the exception of a little nerve pain when I walked, or hobbled I should say.

When I arrived back in Pittsburgh, I took a taxi to the Yough Shore Inn, to pick up my car. I found perpetual guests Delores and her husband sitting just as I left them a week before, and they were just as friendly and charming. They were even dressed the same as they were when I last saw them. She was doing the same crossword puzzles and he was still watching his favorite TV shows. The owner Linn, and Delores, were excited to see me and proceeded to pull out news clippings to show me. Apparently, they had collected stories about my travels the week before, grouped them together in scrap book fashion, and placed them all within the Inn's guestbook. I said my goodbyes, packed up my car and headed out toward my home in northeastern PA. I calculated it would take me about 7 hours. I should get home around 2am, but as it turns out, that didn't go quite as planned.

I got about 2 hours into my drive and realized that my left front calve area was swelling up and felt very strange. It felt like a high pressure water balloon and was beginning to ache and pain. Not ever having this injury before, I became concerned about its root cause, and decided to stop for the night at a hotel west of State College, PA. There, I iced and massaged my leg and slept (tried to) with it elevated up against the headboard of the bed. I ran through different scenarios about the cause and what could happen, in my exhausted overtired state. Was it my bike shoe? Riding position? Was this serious? Bad circulation? Maybe it's a blood clot? I finally fell off to sleep, with my leg still pointing up at the ceiling. The next day the swelling in my leg began to go down and I later determined it was likely a simple case of tendonitis caused by my extreme standing throughout the week. A repetitive use injury of sorts. I had to laugh. My wonky brain had run wild, yet again. So much for trailside enlightenment...My neuroses and I arrived home around lunchtime the following day and received a loving welcome from my family. It was over, I had really done it. Well, not really. It did me, I simply showed up for the ride and learned to let go.

AFTERWORD

How fitting it is to be crafting this Afterword on a St. Patrick's Day weekend, 37 early Sunday morning sessions after beginning this interesting and challenging literary adventure. As I sit huddled up in my favorite coffee shop on a crisp, late winter/early spring morning in rural Pennsylvania, I think back on my very first, significant Standing Cyclist trip in southwest Ireland. I can still see the bright greens and feel the chilly breeze as I move up and down rolling hills and in and out of welcoming villages. I consider my relatively superficial existence before my dad's passing, prior to the 9/11 tragedy, and before my Allergic Asthma diagnosis. I carefully compare that early part of my life with my work-in-progress "second half."

I reflect on how we typically spend our early years surviving and thriving on more of a materialistic, self-centered level, as mentioned earlier in this book. Then, after periods of challenge, responsibility, and sometimes great suffering, some transform and flourish as spiritually oriented, heart-centered beings with a greater focus on the Earth and others around us. Big picture living. We may gain clarity, wisdom and in some traditions, I suspect, a hint of enlightenment. I see now that this first/second half flow of life is by no means a one-way path. We may find ourselves shifting sideways, forward and backward along the route. We are human after all. Imperfection is part of the game. We can only recognize this, for what it is, and keep moving ahead with great patience and strength.

Near the end of the Mesothelioma Challenge, during my final day out on the trail, I reflected on these and many other big ideas and beliefs. In Ireland, way back at the beginning, I had some of these same thoughts but they were so abstract at that time, I couldn't get a grip around them. You could say I had been flirting with wisdom for much of my life. I think most all of us are, much of the time, but until we gain some direct experience and perspective, the details may remain invisible to us. Many of us roll forward, peddling over and around the same obstacles again and again, exhausted, until we realize we've been going around in circles. We may realize this late in life or we may never realize it at all. Some wake up early, course-correct, and recognize the magnificent ride for what it truly is. Just as it is. The sunshine, long summer days, even the rocks, roots, mud and rain, and fellow travelers as well. They are all part of the mix and it's all perfect.

Years ago, I had a passage posted up near my desk. It became a sort of mission statement or mantra. It said, "Do great things, that impact many, in positive ways." I would read it daily through those difficult years of grief, business challenges, and my breathing issues. It meant a great deal to me. During that time, pushing and pushing, I always felt as if I were on the verge of something very important. It was a weird, anxious feeling. It felt oddly right, but something was very wrong. I realize now what it was. I had the right idea, but

I was missing the bigger picture. I was obsessed with and very attached to the results of my actions. I remember moments when I thought, I think I may fail, so why bother? What will people think if I fall short? If I can't make a big difference, why do anything at all? My desktop mantra these days is a bit simpler and way more on the mark, for me at least. It reads, "Simply be. Simply do. Let go." I leave the rest to the natural law of the multiverse. To God, Karma, Ultimate Truth, from a place of openness, boundlessness, unconditional love and deep compassion. I try now to focus only on the doing itself. The rest is clearly none of my business. We can rarely control the results of our actions. There are too many varia-bles, both worldly and spiritual. Why worry about it? Be (authentic), Do (your best), Let go (of results). In this simple, fundamental flow I have found success, peace and fulfillment beyond my wildest imagination.

With each mile I have trained, and each trip I have taken, I have shed a little more unwanted, unneeded gear or baggage along the way. I couldn't hurry through those miles. I couldn't shed too much, too quickly. I had to pace myself and be ok with that pace. I believe we must find our own unique, spe-cial rhythm and continue on in that flow, guilt free. In this way, we remain brave, strong and inspired.

Perseverance and fear come to mind. Very personal topics. When we stop persevering, we stop living. When a cyclist commits to rolling forward, they must pedal, and if they stop, they fall over. What stops us from rolling forward? Fear can be our greatest nemesis is this area, but this is not always obvious to us or those around us. For most all of my life, fears had simmered beneath the surface and have had subtle yet sizeable effects on my navigation. They began when I was a child, afraid to lose my parents. Then, as an adult, afraid to be alone. Later, fears of losing my position in business, my savings, my mobility, and even my mind, would shift my course in life, without ever realizing it on a conscious level. Fears of commitment and personal responsibility would come later still. A shifting, vibrating dread would throttle back my activities but over time our great classroom of life presented me with opportunities, energy and teachings to help me push through this trail mud. The mud didn't dry out entirely. It didn't need to. I embraced it, recognized it for what it was and it became powerless. All I had to do was get out of my own way. I think we can all underestimate just how much damage fear can do. In time, and with clarity and a touch of wisdom, I am now completely convinced we can roll through even the toughest obstacles in our path, with great confidence and success. The kind of clarity and wisdom often gained during the second half of our lives, by fully engaging in every aspect of life itself.

I reflect upon grief and think of my remarkable father. A man of few words while on this Earth in worldly form. We were always very close, but due to his introverted nature, our deep love for one another remained a subtle, rarely demon-strative expression. When I was young, I did not understand his independent, stern, quiet ways but always tried my best to accept him for who he was. Now I can see the pain, worry, balance and wisdom behind his silence. I have experienced some of this first hand, in my own middle age. Since his passing, I feel much closer to him, without any worldly barriers between us. Nothing to insulate his true nature from those of us who remain. In grief I have discovered his silent knowing, like a deep breath of fresh air, and I am grateful. The grief will always exist, but its control over my stance and direction has been completely dismantled.

I cannot help recognize the additional symbolism buried within my last big trip, for Larry Davis. The total trip was long and difficult. Much like the two-part life model described above, it consisted of two different trail sections, ridden one after the other. Each section was exciting, fun, exhausting and painful in their own way, but now that I'm through it, I wouldn't change a thing about either one. Without the unique stirrings of the first, the second would have lacked deep, lasting meaning. When I started the first leg of the trip, I thought I was smarter, kinder, stronger, more authentic and more important than I really was. In my travels, I was beaten down, found inspiration and Rolled on. By the end of the last leg, I was no longer daydreaming about being a standing cyclist or what that meant to me and others. I was The Standing Cyclist, but it no longer mattered, because the "I" no longer mattered. If I could go back and write this book without any of the more than one thousand "I's" used to describe my story, (I) truly would.

So you may be thinking now, what does this all have to do with cycling. The answer is...nothing...and everything. This book represents a journey. An exploration. Inner as well as outer. A transition from plain old fashion flirting, to sleep-walking, to flirting with wisdom. It's not an unusual journey by any means. I was just compelled to write about it, that's all. If you pull something meaningful from it, well, that's quite exciting. If not, then at least you are left with some interesting trailside adventures, until perhaps it's time to read between the lines. No rush.

So, what are my top takeaways? I know now from practical, direct experience that we can in fact "be" and "do" with confidence, without the worry of mistakes. We can live bravely in this present moment, free from the grip of past fears and regrets. We can consciously plan ahead without identifying with worrisome "what if" scenarios. We can engage and attempt to affect positive change, in our lives and the lives of others, with great patience and without identifying with and becoming dependent upon the rush of our own story. We can do, simply for the sake of doing, without attachment to the fruits of our actions. Unconditional, no agenda living. Swimming effortlessly in the big picture of all things, with a perfect stroke.

Yes, my unusual series of mental and physical events, this wild stretch of body, mind and spirit had been experienced and accomplished, but that paled in comparison to the many deeper teachings along the way. Perhaps the greatest for me is that we are all absolutely magnificent, yet quite ordinary, and that is a truly liberating notion.

APPENDIX A

Spotlight Organizations

Throughout my Standing Cyclist journey, so far, it has been my great pleasure to discover many committed fundraisers and activists connected with several special causes and organizations. To learn more about these groups and their missions, please visit them on the web.

Action Against Asbestos
http://www.actionagainstasbestos.com

Asbestos Disease Awareness Organization (ADAO)
http://www.asbestosdiseaseawareness.org

Mesothelioma Applied Research Foundation
http://www.curemeso.org

1% for the Planet
http://www.onepercentfortheplanet.org

Allergy & Asthma Network – Mothers of Asthmatics (AANMA)
http://www.aanma.org

Asthma and Allergy Foundation of America (AAFA)
http://www.aafa.org

Stand Up To Cancer
http://www.standup2cancer.org

Cure SMA (Spinal Muscular Atrophy)
http://www.curesma.org

Safe Haven of Pike County (PA)
http://www.safehavenofpikecounty.org

Peace Jam
http://www.peacejam.org

Food Recovery Network
http://www.foodrecoverynetwork.org

Charity Miles
http://www.charitymiles.org

Bring Change 2 Mind – Ending the Stigma and Discrimination Surrounding Mental Illness
http://bringchange2mind.org

APPENDIX B

Resource Links

For more information on training for and participating in athletic events for a cause, adventure cycling, and health and wellness, please explore:

Team Standing Cyclist
http://www.teamstandingcyclist.com

Frank Angelo Cavaluzzi
http://www.frankangelocavaluzzi.com

Adventure Cycling Association
http://www.adventurecycling.org

International Mountain Biking Association (IMBA)
https://www.imba.com

Exercise is Medicine
http://exerciseismedicine.org

Weil Foundation – Advancing Integrative Medicine
http://www.drweil.com

Wellness Begins Here – Health & Wellness Coaching
http://www.wellnessbeginshere.net

For those of you leaning toward the spiritual, self-exploratory side of life, be sure to visit:

Sounds True – Many Voices, One Journey
http://www.soundstrue.com

Love Serve Remember Foundation – Ram Dass
https://www.ramdass.org

Mind & Life Institute
https://www.mindandlife.org

Center for Action and Contemplation - Richard Rohr
https://cac.org

Plum Village Mindfulness Practice Centre - Thich Nhat Hanh
http://plumvillage.org

Spirit Rock Meditation Center
http://www.spiritrock.org

In loving memory of...

Tristin Marie Buckstad

August 20, 1970 – January 24, 2014

May your challenges fall aside leaving only peace
and freedom ahead. May that spark of love
and fiery wisdom, that is your very essence,
never be extinguished.

ABOUT THE AUTHOR

Frank Angelo Cavaluzzi continues to train and tour for special causes, world-wide, in his typical Standing Cyclist fashion. When he's not leading complex marketing and engineering programs and projects for innovative businesses, and maintaining TeamStandingCyclist.com, Frank proudly serves as a www.CharityMiles.org Ambassador. In September of 2016, he rode 369 miles across New York State (#StandingNY) to promote Charity Miles and their groundbreaking, highly rated athletic fundraising App. No coasting, no sitting. For 10 days he recruited new App users and logged miles for Feeding America, an important non-profit organization which helps feed millions of starving people in the U.S. every year.